Parents and Teachers Together

Innovations in Education

Series Editor: Colin Fletcher (Reader in the School of Policy Studies, Cranfield Institute of Technology).

There have been periods of major innovation in public education. What do the achievements amount to and what are the prospects for progress now? There are issues in each slice of the education sector. How have the issues come about?

Each author analyses their own sphere, argues from experience and communicates clearly. Here are books that speak both with and for the teaching profession; books that can be shared with all those involved in the future of education.

Three quotations have helped to shape the series:

The whole process – false starts, frustrations, adaptations, the successive recasting of intentions, the detours and conflicts – needs to be comprehended. Only then can we understand what has been achieved and learn from experience.

Marris and Rein

In this time of considerable educational change and challenge the need for teachers to write has never been greater.

Hargreaves

A wise innovator should prepare packages of programmes and procedures which . . . could be put into effect quickly in periods of recovery and reorganisation following a disaster.

Hirsh

Titles in the series

Parents and Teachers Together

Partnership in Primary and Nursery Education

Mary Stacey

Open University Press
Milton Keynes · Philadelphia

Open University Press
Celtic Court
22 Ballmoor
Buckingham
MK18 1XW

and
1900 Frost Road, Suite 101
Bristol, PA 19007, USA

First published 1991

British Library Cataloguing in Publication Data

Stacey, Mary
    Parents and teachers together: partnership in primary and nursery
    education.
    1. Great Britain. Schools. Relations with parents
    I. Title
    371.103941
    ISBN 0-335-09436-8
    ISBN 0-335-09435-X (pbk.)

Library of Congress Cataloging-in-Publication Data

Stacey, Mary, 1943–
    Parents and teachers together: partnership in primary and nursery
    education/Mary Stacey.
        p.   cm.
    Includes bibliography (p. 120) and index.
    ISBN 0-335-09436-8.—ISBN 0-335-09435-X (pbk.)
    1. Parent–teacher relationships—Great Britain.   2. Education,
    Elementary—Great Britain—Parent participation.   3. Education,
    Preschool—Great Britain—Parent participation.   I. Title.
    LC225.33.G7S73   1991
    372.11′03′0941—dc20   90-14237
                                                                    CIP

Typeset by Rowland Phototypesetting Ltd
Bury St Edmunds, Suffolk
Printed in Great Britain by
St Edmundsbury Press Ltd, Bury St Edmunds, Suffolk

Contents

Series editor's introduction

Few teachers begin their professional life by being parents themselves. Most have left the parental home quite recently. Among student teachers there are lots of conversations about their own childhood, and indeed their own parents. Student teachers, meanwhile, learn formally about subjects and curricula, about children and what schools might be like. A world image is being created. With the help of this book the image should now include the children's parents and what Linnea Timson calls the 'family as a learning environment'. There will no longer be a need or excuse for the shock of dealing with parents from the moment of becoming a proper teacher.

In time, too, teachers, often do become parents themselves. Then they vary considerably as to how close or distant they are from their own children's school or 'education'. Yet it is fascinating how teachers can still talk about children as if their parents did not exist, whether they be straight from initial training or actually parents themselves.

Mary Stacey makes a window in this wall of make-believe. She writes equally about parents and teachers, and carefully separates the strands of being a parent and being a teacher. She has decades of participation and observation: as a preschool centre head, through postgraduate research, by being a trainer and from penetrating scholarship. Her book has neither prejudice nor special pleading. This is a delicate and close study of the contacts and communications that can happen – and some that should. The attitudes and actions are brought out through theory, discussed as themes and given examples. Each chapter is signposted clearly and written (as Socrates suggested) with force, ease and clarity.

The problems of both teacher and parent are such that sharing aspects of their understanding can lessen the load. But that is not the most important point. Stacey shows that the point is the common welfare of the child. It is as simple as a joy shared is a joy enjoyed, an achievement through an appreciation of each and every child. That is the difference: the parent knows *his* or *her child* and the teacher knows *some* children. The difference between the singular and the general remains and can be a strength.

Political and demographic changes have made parents more 'important'. There is universally more involvement in the government of schools, the long-term consequences of which are unknown. So far there has been a mixture of loyalty and interfering expertise, traditionalism, progressivism and indifference. The business model of involvement is much in evidence – budgets, cost codes and cash limits. Governors are given the mistaken identity of a Board of Directors. So it is the political model which will shape involvement, too – parties, constituencies, and manifestos. The demography of there being fewer children increases all parents' power as 'consumers'. They become more choosy. It costs a lot to bring up a child. There is no reason to think that money spent by the majority on children is easily earned and without heartache. The models become still more significant if one thinks of the political economy of parenting. All schools will find they are expected to know the business and political models. Teachers will find them full of dark threats *and* of little use when they really meet parents.

So Stacey enables the *lived* experience of teachers and parents. She gives careful thought to the literature and helpful attention to useful exercises and role play. Teachers must be properly prepared to deal with parents. They must practise what they are going to say and do. So many mistakes can be made. So many good moves can be almost as easily made.

I found the idea of teaching being 'mothering made conscious' the most challenging, or perhaps it is the way Stacey works it out which makes it truly memorable. Above all, I appreciated the scope of this book: the feel of schools, the sounds of relationships and the pre-eminent good sense of partnership with parents.

Colin Fletcher

Acknowledgements

First I should like to thank the many parents and the staff who, during my years at South Harringay, taught me so much. Thanks, too, to the headteachers who welcomed me into their schools when I was doing my thesis into parent–teacher partnership. I am grateful to them as well as to the teachers, parents, advisers, education officers and community workers who spent time talking about what parental involvement meant for them. Finally, I wish to thank all those who gave particular help and encouragement while I was writing the book: Julie Cotter, Chris Driver, Sheranie Qaisar, Kim Suleyman, Wai Li Tan and Aicha Touassi, who helped me touch base again with their comments as parents; Rita Miller, James Shepherd, David Silverman, Alison Steer and Dorothy Wedge, for their discussions or for comments on the first drafts; Pamela Johnson, Gillian Lacey, Sue Lewis and Esther Stacey, who gave me much support during the dark times of writing; and Colin Fletcher, who kept moving me on to the light at the end of the tunnel.

PART I

Why involve parents?

Looking at what parental involvement means to me has been like a 'restless, impatient, continuing, hopeful inquiry' (Freire 1972). It has been restless and impatient because, as I have learnt, the process is too complex, too dynamic to find easy answers. As a realist and practitioner, I believe that idealistic myths and vague notions of parent–teacher partnership and community compatibility become obstructive. Developing relationships with people takes time; structures can inhibit; we make mistakes. But, as an optimist, I also find the inquiry is continuing and hopeful. Once we understand the conflicts, the barriers and our limitations we can also acknowledge our strengths and all that we can offer each other. Then we can work together for the child and for children.

Part I begins with my experience of working closely with parents and traces the background to parental involvement since the 1960s. It then looks at the present roles of teacher and parent and how these are changing.

CHAPTER 1

Beginnings

'I don't come every day, but I just like to know it's there.'

(Parent)

A bomb had gone off in the Turkish bank down the road. It was my first morning in a new job. I had been appointed to set up an educational resource centre – a drop-in centre for parents and preschool children. I looked at the old Victorian building with its concrete steps and the two rooms piled high with rubbish. It was definitely not purpose-built. One would certainly not choose it as a centre for young children, nor was it a homely welcoming kind of building which would encourage people to call in. But somebody in the education department had been successful in getting an urban aid grant for this project and had found some empty rooms in a block next to a school. It was 1978. Linking the home and school and working more closely with the community was high on the agenda.

I went to see the headteacher at the school next door. She smiled: 'No, I haven't been involved in the planning. I don't know how you'll get on. I think you'll find it pretty difficult in this area. If people aren't at work, they're working at home.' I had the energy which comes with getting a new job and I had learnt a lot as an educational visitor elsewhere. I had grown used to working on the periphery of a school instead of in the classroom so although my enthusiasm was dinted I was not daunted.

Later on, I met the head of the adult literacy unit, based in the same building where the centre was to be. He was worried. 'Yes, I did hear you were coming. What are you going to be doing exactly? I hope it will be all right. What about the toilets – I don't think our students will like having the children in there.'

It was not an encouraging start. But what I faced on that first day is unlikely to be very different from what many people setting up a new project involving schools and parents will find today. There is not usually overwhelming enthusiasm. Schools running smoothly and efficiently for the children, as this one was, do not want to be upset by extra people and groups of parents. Other organizations worry about how they will be affected if they have not been involved in the planning. Sharing resources – particularly toilets – is not easy. The community itself is not usually homogeneous. There is conflict out there and if you begin to bring diverse members of the community together, there are bound to be differences of opinion at all levels – educationally, socially and politically.

Theory into practice

The setting up of the South Harringay Preschool Centre had been inspired by the action research carried out from 1969 to 1971 in the West Riding of Yorkshire, one of five designated educational priority areas (EPAs). The rationale underlying this research was that it was more a lack of knowledge than of interest which led to the disparity between middle-class and working-class achievement and that this could be rectified by 'involving the community more closely in the educational process' (Halsey 1972). The director of one of the other projects, in Liverpool, Midwinter (1977), saw the need for 'ordinariness to be made articulate'. By looking first at the educational needs of a particular community the structures could then adapt and what was presented to the children could become much more relevant.

The 1970s were optimistic days in the community education movement. Halsey's community school model was to 'obliterate the boundary between school and community, to turn the community into a school and the school into a community'. Midwinter went further; he believed in an 'educative community' with education becoming 'more like everything else'. At the same time as the Halsey Report, Mrs Thatcher, the then Secretary of State for Education, presented the government White Paper *Education: a Framework for Expansion* (Department of Education and Science (DES) 1972). It stressed the need for nursery education on demand, especially in EPA, and encouraged a more flexible approach to preschooling. There was talk of a much more democratic system, with education authorities and teachers becoming more accessible. Yet it meant, as Midwinter pointed out, an enormous reform in teacher training:

> The community school has to be involved in changing and not standing still. Teachers will have to become the social prosecutors

rather than the social defenders if the school is, in effect, to shift itself massively and become a positive influence on social change.

Research into parental involvement had mainly focused on the preschool years. It seemed a natural place to work with parents. The role of the mother was constantly under scrutiny. Bowlby's (1953) theories on the crucial relation of early maternal care and children's mental health were still extremely influential; at the same time women were demanding the right to work and questioning the nature of the mothering role. The playgroup movement had established itself as a major force in preschool education and was demonstrating visibly how parents could run their own groups and be involved in their children's learning.

With this background in mind, the centre was set up to provide an 'informal children's centre for preschool children and their parents or surrogate parents'. As the school had a part-time nursery class, it was envisaged that the children making use of the facility would probably be between 18 months and 3½ years. The decision had been made to set it up outside the school system and, as I had discovered, with little consultation with those who would be immediately affected.

Pugh and De'Ath (1984) pointed out the enormous variety of approaches and number of experts in the field of early child care and education. They listed the many names used by those who work with parents: 'preparation for parenthood, family life education, parentcraft, parent training, mothercraft, parent education, education for family life and parents as educators'. In the 1960s, there had been much emphasis on intervention. Headstart, in the United States, aimed its much publicized programme at 'disadvantaged' preschool children, believing that with highly structured learning programmes their IQ level would be raised and they would perform more effectively in school. It started with massive resources and optimism. The short-term effects were limited; the long-term ones were hard to assess since the 'success' itself was difficult to define and measure. Nevertheless, what became clear, highlighted some years later, was the importance of parents' active participation in the programmes. Although, from the data available, it was not possible to give precise reasons, many of the long-term effects were a result of parent–child interaction and not teacher–child interaction as had been expected (Bronfenbrenner 1974).

By the 1970s, the emphasis was beginning to shift towards 'information' rather than 'intervention'. Certainly for those of us working closely with parents and children in their homes as well as at school, it soon became evident that it was we as teachers who needed to adapt our role, to develop a more informal and flexible approach; we were as much a part of the learning process as the parents and children. We had information to share and support to give but it was arrogant to tell parents how to bring up their children. We saw at first hand parents – some of whom were under tremendous pressure and facing difficulties that we had never experienced – as a major learning resource and main influence in their children's lives.

The staff appointed to the centre were all committed to the idea of working much more closely with parents but none had received any formal training in working with adults. They believed that parents should be actively involved in their children's education, although what this meant proved to be a fairly vague concept and it took time to understand the implications. We were to encourage 'mothers and surrogate parents to use the facilities provided and to assist them in identifying their needs'. The resources were ourselves, the building, toys and equipment, and, as we were soon to learn, other parents and people in the neighbourhood. The 'needs' in a culturally and socially diverse community were various and not always immediately identifiable.

It had also been stressed that the 'educational emphasis would be on developing strategies for learning rather than a single short term language programme'. There had been great emphasis on the importance of children's language in the 1960s and 1970s. Much of the research and debate had centred on the inadequacies of working-class language. Bernstein's (1971) theories of language in socialization and education fuelled the controversy. He highlighted the relationship between social class and the way language is used; he distinguished between the 'restricted' code of working-class children and the 'elaborated' code of middle-class children and drew attention to the working-class child's inability to communicate in the middle-class setting of the school. Tough (1973), in her work on language and young children, had emphasized the teacher's crucial role in child language development. She argued that the teacher could be the only source of help for 'disadvantaged' children and, seeing it as essentially a professional task to give children appropriate linguistic experiences, developed in-service programmes for teachers to help with children's language in school (Tough 1979). The Bullock Report (DES 1975) also perceived the language of the 'culturally disadvantaged' home as 'limited by certain norms of relationship' and advocated health visitors and educational visitors to help parents 'bathe their children in language' before they came to school.

Bernstein (1970) argued that he was being misinterpreted and that he was emphasizing the 'differences' not the 'deficiencies'. But the deficit model pervaded much of the educational thinking of the time with the stress on compensation. Bernstein criticized compensatory education as a means of 'directing attention away from the internal organization and educational context of the school'. Wells (1978) drew attention to the 'closed' nature of many of the conversations children have with teachers in school. And Bruner (1974) challenged the simplistic notion that teachers alone could overcome the 'disadvantage', pointing out that 'being socio-economically disadvantaged is no simple matter of deficit, of suffering a cultural avitaminosis that can be dosed by suitable inputs of compensation'.

As Tomlinson (1984) has pointed out, it was unfortunate that many children from minority homes were entering school for the first time when models of working-class failure and disadvantage were popular. Their culture, even when recognized as different, quickly became stereotyped; the idea of non-academic West Indians and hard-working Asians with unrealistic academic aspirations became common myths which still persist (DES 1985a) and much of the research emphasized the problematic nature of teachers relating to these parents. Although the Plowden Report (DES 1967) recommended that contacts with 'immigrant' parents were especially important, it noted that these were 'far from easy to establish' and highlighted the language barrier. Bullock (DES 1975), too, although underlining the importance of children retaining cultural and linguistic difference, stressed the difficulty of contact and dialogue between parents and teachers:

> Mothers may be at work all day, or live in purdah, or speak no English; fathers may be permanently on night shift. Notices from school are sometimes not read or are misinterpreted. The parents sometimes want to delegate to the school full responsibility of social training.

Children were still being referred to as 'non-English speaking'; the advantage of being bilingual was not stressed. Yet we saw children of three and four understanding what language to speak to whom and when. It was we who were at the disadvantage.

It was evident that during the preschool years parents and children could be involved with many different agencies. Thus another aim of the centre was to 'provide a resource which could be used by many agencies involved with the preschool child and parents'. There had been a representative from social services at my interview but this was not a jointly set up project so when others were interviewed they never came again. Other departments always regarded the education department as the one with money and resources. And it has to be said that there was not a tradition of sharing.

It was individual workers who got involved. Health visitors referred families to us that they thought would be interested. But they were worried at first about doing this. After all, the health service itself did not usually reveal its clients to other agencies. After some years, a social worker and housing adviser came at a regular time so that people could have easy access to them. The head of the adult literacy centre whom I had met on the first day became a friend and supporter but there was never any formal agreement between the adult education department and the schools department. We worked closely together because we were in the same building and saw how much we had in common and how effective we could be as a joint resource. We even bought a photocopier together, although the procedure to fund this jointly was extremely complicated and it was never clear who should pay for the servicing!

Some workers were more interested than others but we began to build a network in the area. Childminders came into the centre and parents could get to know who was in the neighbourhood. As time went on, we developed trust between the different workers. This was essential if parents were to trust us. We were visiting some parents regularly at home, taking toys and activities in to the children and spending time with the parents. This could be for all sorts of reasons: sometimes women working at home found it difficult to come out; some wanted extra support or a child had a developmental delay. Sometimes health visitors or social workers would refer us to families and it was absolutely essential that parents knew why we were there and could decide whether we came or not. We had, after all, no statutory right to be there.

We worked closely with the Home Intervention Scheme (HINTS), which visited children with special needs and used the Portage model as its framework. Staff from the centre began to visit families regularly. At first they worried that using Portage might be too restricting but soon realized that this did not have to be purely child-focused and that they could be flexible and holistic in their approach. They appreciated the supervision with the social worker who co-ordinated this project. 'Supervision', being a social work term, can be misunderstood in education and often has a connotation of overseeing rather than support. But they found that the opportunity to analyse what they were doing and bounce ideas off each other was helpful to them as well as those with whom they were working. Parents appreciated the child-centred approach: 'It was a guideline for us. It taught us what to do with him.' But they also liked working as equal adults: 'we talked and talked – I told her what I felt – I trusted her . . . she wasn't shallow and mechanical'(Silverman and Stacey 1989). We found that sharing our perspectives about the children gave both parent and worker a more rounded picture.

The final aim of the project was that parents 'share in the decision making'. The original submission for the grant stated:

> Bernstein and Bruner have pointed out how important it is that parents share in the decision making power particularly in the preschool field, and ultimately a management committee of users would report to the Schools Sub-Committee on the use of the centre.

These were fine words, but the reality was very different. On a personal level or day-to-day basis it was possible to discuss ideas and come to decisions together. But structurally, there was much that inhibited the 'power'. As staff, we were employees of the education authority. We had fixed salaries, hours and budget. Decision-making could involve how we spent our time and what we did in the centre. But it took several years before the authority accepted parents on the interviewing panel for new staff. It was significant that the first time there was a ballot for a parent representative, someone who had been in teaching was chosen. 'She knows how to do things' was the general opinion. Others did not see themselves as being able to offer much; they needed a lot of convincing about their value if 'experts' were going to be there.

Only a few parents were interested in being on committees. The schools sub-committee met at a time when people were generally putting children to bed. When we submitted our first report, we waited until 10.30 p.m. before it appeared on the agenda. It was obvious that only a few councillors had read it and all was over in five minutes. Rallying support for those kinds of committee is not easy. If this is seen as 'decision making power' most parents with very young children quite understandably are not very interested, nor do they have the energy to take on lots of extra commitments. Our emphasis had to be on getting information across both on an individual level and in groups; we had to do this always, not just at set times.

Getting started

So the aims were laid down: the words on paper before a project starts and people actually get involved. There was a community out there, a school next door, neither of which had been consulted. The community was a truly multicultural one; there were at least twenty ethnic groups and many different languages spoken. Clearly, to encourage people to use the facilities and say what they wanted was going to take time; those of us who worked there would need a real understanding of the community. The idea of a place that you dropped into when it suited you was a completely new concept. It was not a nursery where you left the children and there were parents who were looking for full-day care. There were those who felt extremely shy about coming into a group. What would be expected of them and their children? Some spoke little or no English and we only had one member of staff who was bilingual.

All the staff – except the clerical assistant, a local parent – were teachers or nursery nurses; some of us had come straight from the classroom. Although we were now outside the school, we had to do what all teachers have to do who want to work more closely with parents. We had to examine our practice with the children since we were always under the scrutiny of the parents. We had to challenge our preconceived ideas about childrearing. We had to explain, and sometimes justify, the activities we put on and to become more flexible in our timing and organization.

But above all, we had to look at how we related to parents as 'professionals'. We had to face our prejudices and differences, and it was not always easy. We had to learn to accept criticism. One of the first lessons we learnt was to 'be' rather than always to 'do'. We began to adapt to a place that had no definite routine; people came and went when it suited them. Sometimes there were only two or three parents and children; at other times the place was bursting at the seams. The age range in the room could vary from a few weeks to late seventies. Although we usually put on activities for small children, the holidays brought an influx of older sisters and brothers who wanted something different. So we began to think in terms of families rather than individual children.

We learnt to relax and to listen. There were people who wanted to talk things out. Because we believed that listening to children and adults is even more important than talking to them, people began to know and trust us. They began to realize that what was said to the staff would neither be judged nor go further. Yet remarks, which came from parents and visiting teachers, such as 'you have such an easy job, sitting around all day and the parents are always there' were not always easy to take. We knew that although it may be tiring it is often much simpler to work only with children. In the classroom we were the undisputed boss; we could make the rules, organize and set the pace. With parents about, we had to be aware of their relationship with their children and the importance of this. Parents were not always clear of their role in relation to us. And the question of responsibility had to be addressed. Perhaps one of the most vexed questions was who does the washing up and tidying away. After all, we were the paid workers, yet we believed everybody should help!

Certainly, in the setting in which we worked, it was not only possible but natural to step out of the role of teacher. Many of the preconceptions that people have about schools did not exist. The children were very young; parents were not surprised if they 'played all day' as they sometimes are when this seems to happen in the infant school. But working in an informal setting where boundaries are not clearly specified can bring other dilemmas. It means taking a flexible approach, being clear of the overall aims but ready to adapt to what is brought in. Sometimes the focus was entirely on the children but there were other times when individual parent's needs took precedence.

All the staff found that it took time to adapt. The idea at first was that parents coming into the centre joined in the activities with their children. It was not long before staff realized that many parents did not come in for this. They came in for a break, to meet other adults, to talk about what was going on in their lives. This did not mean that they were not interested in what their children were doing; but they preferred to watch at times rather than take an active part. Once the centre was really established as a place where you could relax, women would sometimes fall asleep: I remember two very pregnant women, both with their feet up on the sofas as their other children played around them. 'He wouldn't leave me alone at home. I feel I can rest here,' said one. This was not the kind of parent involvement we so often expect when we ask parents in to be with their children at school. But it was realistic. We knew that people were concerned; they talked about what their children were doing, learning, and how they were progressing. There were times when they sat down with them and played with jigsaws or dough or read to them. But they had needs as adults as well. Indeed, people wanted a break sometimes, so we set up times when they could leave their children. Many made friends with other adults, and they began to take care of each other's children.

At the beginning we spent a lot of time inviting people directly. We visited them at home to tell them who we were, what the centre was offering. We met women and children in the street. Sometimes people apologized when they had not come regularly. But gradually they began to realize that they could come when they wanted. We became aware of the times of day when it was easy for people to come. It depended on children's sleeping patterns, partners' shift work, family or work commitments and whether what was happening at the centre was of interest. I suggested to a Cypriot grandmother, who apologized for not speaking much English, that she might like to come to the language classes we put on. She could speak well enough to tell me that she had lived twenty years in the neighbourhood: she shopped in the Greek shops, she had Greek friends, so she believed she could manage without my advice. She became a regular user and supporter of the centre, bringing grandchildren and those she was minding. She was also always ready to come to any celebration or party and I learnt the lesson that I do not necessarily know what is 'right' for people.

People arranged to come when their friends or someone who spoke their language was there. Sometimes they avoided neighbours or people they did not like. There were problems, particularly at the beginning, with cliques forming. This is divisive in any area but particularly in a multicultural one. It can easily put people off coming and is uncomfortable for everyone, including the workers. We did not find it easy to deal with except that we made it quite clear that we were not part of these groups, that everyone was equally welcome, and we had to challenge groups at certain times. As staff and users gained confidence and as the centre became established these cliques began to disappear.

There was also racism within the groups which we had to be constantly aware of. It was not always expressed overtly. For instance, one woman came in, looked round the room, saw only Asian and Cypriot women and left, muttering: 'Oh, there's nobody here'. There were preconceived ideas about children and there were definite differences in childrearing practices. But one of the greatest advantages of working with the adults as well as children is that attitudes can change. Many of the myths can be dispelled as people get to know each other, exchange ideas, acknowledge differences and share their concerns about bringing up children.

It was not always comfortable to be at the centre. There were people who were difficult and there were differences of opinion. There were some splendid rows and some awkward silences when people fell out with each other. Sometimes we had to intervene, particularly if it was interfering with what was happening. But when to use my 'authority' was always a dilemma. With very young children, arguments between parents could easily erupt because of a child's behaviour. It needed a lot of understanding on both sides and left parents feeling very vulnerable. A mother who was particularly distressed by her child's 'aggressive' behaviour went on the defensive, feeling she had to leave the group. Yet, as she realized, it was important for him to meet other children and she needed support to bring him along. At first this came from the staff but as time went on and other parents had been through the same kind of experience, they were also able to reassure or suggest strategies to help.

Sometimes arguments were nothing to do with us. They were about adults making and breaking relationships, letting out their bad feelings, feeling frustrated. What we had to make sure was that, whatever happened, people were still welcome and were valid members of the group. They had children who needed to be cared for and have opportunities to play like the rest. We had to learn to become less controlling – which is hard if you have been trained to avoid conflict and create a 'happy' atmosphere in primary or nursery schools. Conflict is never easy to deal with, yet it is inevitable if there is to be change and people are able to express what they think. What we found important was the support that we could give to each other when we were caught up in others' anger or distress.

Moving on

The first few years were certainly the most difficult but also the most exciting as the place evolved and took off as a focal point in the neighbourhood. As the years went by, people began to feel proud of being part of a multicultural community. They exchanged ideas. This started with bringing in food and swapping recipes as it so often does, but it moved on from there. Bringing up children in an urban area brought common problems. There was shared grief when a young mother died, but there was also much celebration when babies were born. 'We're keeping the centre going with all these births – there'll always be a job for you round here' was the joke. We organized a summer festival. There was Greek, Irish, Indian and English country dancing, a steel band, African drumming; children and adults took part. We looked at each others' photographs and artefacts; we sent balloons up into the air hoping people would find them elsewhere and know we were there. It was a positive demonstration of the many different cultures from which we came.

Groups came and went. Classes and discussion groups evolved over the years, depending on needs and interests. The English classes always continued and after some years we were able to employ bilingual parents as the crèche workers. This helped the children and parents attending and also gave some people an opportunity to earn some money. People began to attend the literacy classes – they knew that their children would be well looked after. Sometimes it took courage to go; sometimes people made several false starts. After a few years, a maths group began. This was taught by a mother who had been a maths teacher. Again the crèche workers were women from the centre and the appointment of people that they knew and trusted made it much easier for people to join the classes.

Skills were varied and often kept hidden. We had several exhibitions of adult work. There was a regular craft group where people not only brought ideas but were also introduced to activities such as batik, silk-painting and crocheting. They could work at their own pace and level. At the exhibitions, people would bring in things which had been handed down in the family or intricate work which none of us had realized they could do. The amazement and admiration of others was important, particularly for women who would constantly put themselves down by saying 'I'm just a mum'.

With young children, it is easy to feel isolated and a loss of identity. It was mainly women who came, although a few fathers and grandparents dropped in, and having a male worker for a while made it less obviously women's work to bring up children. We believed it was important to recognize people as adults not just as 'somebody's mum'. The children were always there. It was the reason why people came to the centre – at least that is what people said initially. But as one mother, attending a class, put it: 'to have two hours where I can concentrate on things other than the family is just great'.

There were people living in bed and breakfast places, there were those who were depressed, going through marriage breakups and illness. It would be easy to concentrate on the parents with the 'problems' in this description. But as important is to acknowledge that in these situations people continued to show courage and strength. Despite these difficulties they still wanted the best for their children. We learnt that we did not have all the answers. We had certain skills to offer, we learnt to facilitate; but it was the users who made things happen in the end. At one group discussion, I suggested we had an 'expert' come in. 'What do we want people who write books for,' one mother commented, 'we have each other now'. And certainly there is tremendous knowledge and wisdom within any group of women; it is a resource which is often underestimated and left untapped.

Staff introduced many of the activities and ideas. Sometimes these were taken over by parents. But some parents just wanted a base; a few stayed all day and every day – because they did not want to be at home. There were increasing numbers of childminders who found the centre a useful resource for toys, play and support. Some people came in and took up the adult education options. Others used it primarily as a toddlers' group and some simply came in for information. For whatever use, people wanted it; the centre was a focal point for children and adults. It became an exchange and mart for goods and, more importantly, for information. If we did not know the answer, we tried to find out or asked others. A lot of what happened was not visible nor easily definable – for instance, the influences that people had on each other, the raising of self-esteem, the information which started someone off on a new route.

People learnt more about children. They saw their own within a group, made comparisons; they sometimes realized that they were not the only one who had a 'really naughty' child or one who never slept. They used and borrowed toys and books, asked about suppliers. They got to know other people's children and saw them growing up, going to school, changing. They began to find out how the education system worked. First it was the school: what did they do there? Was it a good one? What were the teachers like? This was not easy for the school. Dinner supervisors did not enjoy parents looking over the fence to see how their children were settling in or playing, although it did make a difference when some of the parents who had been at the centre got such jobs. People began to ask each other's opinions. A mother came in extremely angry one day because her child had been told off. She was all for going to give the headteacher 'a piece of her mind'. Some of her friends began to make her talk through what had happened. She still went to the head, but not in a rage. She went with some specific questions of why the incident had happened.

Parents began to make more demands on the school. They wanted

to be more involved. They had developed very informal relationships with us. Anyone who came into the centre was not expected to
stand on ceremony. There was always considerable mirth when
'people from the office' came 'looking posh in their suits'. An HMI
who spent the day with us suggested that he should come in his
jeans. It was a good idea. It was the first time, he said, that he had
been to work dressed like that although he still looked smart! It was
not actually the clothes that made the difference but his attitude. He
was not trying to come down to their level but ridding himself of the
authority image. He had no difficulty in spending the day talking
with parents and he even went on a visit with the educational visitor.
Women gave him their views on the centre, their children, local
schools and life in general. He learnt a great deal more than many of
the visitors who only really felt comfortable talking to the staff in a
space away from the users.

Pugh *et al.* (1987) describes a school which had been involved in
setting up a parents' drop-in centre next to it and the hopes of the
headteacher that parents would be 'empowered to challenge the
school from a position of strength and understanding'. As she points
out, this is not always easy in reality; she writes:

> the increasing confidence exhibited by some parents as a result of
> working in the parents' centre and nursery, is in some cases
> creating rather than solving problems, as parents develop a view
> of their role which is not always in accord with what some
> teachers had hoped for.

We, too, began to find ourselves in a difficult position. Some of
the nursery teachers wanted parents to stay, but they found it
annoying when they did not conform or take on a specific helping
role. Many parents preferred to stay with the centre because they felt
more at ease and in control. As staff, we were often asked to 'deal'
with parents especially when it meant making a visit or looking into
an awkward situation because 'you know them better than us'.

Change is always gradual. Over the years, staff came and went
both at the school and at the centre – and so did parents. But as the
children we had known moved into the junior school and then on to
secondary school, we saw parents taking on active roles as governors, playgroup leaders, mother-tongue teachers. They were
prepared to write to councillors when the centre was under threat.
The junior school headteacher, having not long been appointed,
came to one of the family parties held in his hall because we had
outgrown our room. There were children of all ages, families from

all sorts of different ethnic groups, people who had moved away and come back to see old friends. The hall was packed out, noisy but alive. 'They feel together,' he said, 'it's a natural thing for the kids and parents to be here.'

Those of us who worked at the centre felt we had learnt more in that period about education than at any other time. Many parents saw it as an important time in their lives, too. We learnt from each other, supported each other and, above all, joined together for the benefit of the child. The focus may have appeared to be primarily on the adults at times but that was because we believed that parenting is rarely given the status it deserves; it is often dismissed as something everybody is expected to do whatever their circumstances. Yet as the Children's Committee (1980) suggested, society has a 'responsibility to ensure that parents are afforded access to help, advice and support in bringing up their children, not just to combat particular moments of severe and identifiable vulnerability, but also to deal with the common concerns of life'.

It is difficult to be objective and report the 'hard facts' about a project when you have been so much part of it. There were those critics who said to us: 'It's all right for you – you work full-time with parents. You don't have a school to run.' This was true, and certainly some of the barriers in school did not exist for us. Staff who left to go back to work as teachers in the classroom came up against restrictions such as time and organization. But they learnt that the same principles apply wherever you are working. Parents and workers have to develop trust and respect for each other. They need to acknowledge their different but equally valid skills and abilities and use these together for the children. There often have to be radical changes in attitudes; this can be painful and disruptive. But research is consistently showing that parents and teachers working together in many different ways does benefit the children. It must, then, be worth trying. When the opportunity to do a piece of research about parents and teachers came up I decided it was time I went back into school to see if what I believed in could happen there.

CHAPTER 2

Teachers – accountable to whom?

'The last thing you want is your child's teacher upset and they think you're a really pushy parent treading on their toes.'

(Parent)

Most countries do not have a tradition of close home–school relations; with a few exceptions, teachers have expected parents to assign the children to them during school time without interference. They have not been the 'would-be missionaries awaiting a lead to stimulate parental interest' (Roberts 1980). Research and government reports on the other hand have called repeatedly for greater links between home and school.

The Plowden Report (DES 1967), one of the most influential and best known on primary schools, suggested a minimum requirement of involvement. This included welcoming parents into school, organizing meetings, arranging open days, making information available and giving reports to parents. Many schools have carried out these suggestions to a greater or lesser extent. But it has remained up to the teachers to decide how far this involvement should go. The report was quite clear that parents should not 'run the schools'.

Conditions of service

Since the nature of the commitment to parents has always remained a voluntary one, what has happened has depended largely on the interest of individual teachers and the headteacher. The diffuse nature of the role was evident in the *Conditions of Service* (Council of Local Education Authorities 1978), which emphasized the voluntary nature of the teacher's duties, stating that 'there are no national collective agreements in defining the teacher's day, duties and holiday entitlement' and that 'the success of these activities depends on the extent and quality of the voluntary efforts of individual teachers under the leadership of the headteacher'. Thus teachers needed to feel no compulsion to join in extra-curricular activities or attend out-of-school staff meetings or in-service training and much of the onus rested with the headteacher. Since most of the activities with parents were deemed 'voluntary', schools varied tremendously in how they interpreted their 'duties'. 'Goodwill' was seen as an integral part of what they did.

During the 1980s, there was bitter confrontation between the teachers' unions and the government as the role and conditions of service were radically changed. Teachers withdrew their 'goodwill' several times during industrial disputes. The autonomy which they valued and had fought hard to keep was profoundly altered. Teachers' negotiating rights, set up through the Burnham Committee in 1926, were diminished. There are now clear definitions of their day and duty. The curriculum, which has always remained in the hands of the teachers and has been jealously guarded as part of their professionalism, is now laid down in the Education Reform Act 1988. The voluntary nature of their role has virtually disappeared, partly because of the new conditions and partly because much of the 'goodwill' has gone – possibly for ever. Parents have a very different role to play as governors with powers to manage and control.

All this has had a considerable effect on most teachers' view of their role and responsibilities to parents. Many were exhausted by the amount of new information they had to absorb. The speed with which new legislation was introduced left them stunned. They grappled with new ideas, feeling that they had little time to digest them. Change is never easy and many felt under stress as colleagues left the profession, resources decreased, and a completely new way of managing school finances was introduced. It is no wonder that some felt undermined by parents expressing their views at governors' meetings and resentful that they had to give up time to them when they had their work cut out teaching the children. The numbers in some classes increased and the priority quite naturally for most teachers was to introduce new schemes of work and ways of assessment demanded by the government.

According to Cyster *et al.* (1979) parents were seen by most teachers as 'an additional and avoidable complication in an already demanding life'. Not a lot has changed, except that the role with parents is less 'avoidable'. Teachers are now required to give parents an annual curriculum plan giving 'details of attainment targets in the forthcoming year'. They need 'to be able to present to other teachers and the parents concerned throughout any given key stage, basic *data* on how any given pupil is progressing within any given attainment target' (DES 1989b).

Previous discussions with parents could – and often did – revolve around vague concepts of how a child was getting on. It was possible to say that a child was 'happy' or 'trying hard' without referring to what he or she had actually accomplished. Some parents would only expect five or ten minutes at the open evening and, since they were not used to discussions with teachers, were often relieved that they did not go on longer. Teachers, outwardly complaining that as usual it was only the interested ones who turned up, were sometimes secretly glad about this.

The specific attainment targets which teachers are now obliged to talk about with parents can give a focus to the discussion. But the way they explain or interpret these will have a tremendous effect on how a parent receives the information. The child is not an isolated being but comes into school with a culture and experience which cannot be ignored. How the teacher sees the parent's role, responsibility and influence on the child's progress will certainly have an impact on the outcome of the communication.

Ironically, although good communication is at the heart of any teacher's job, the main emphasis in initial and in-service training is usually on the children's language and not so much on the teacher's. The importance of being able to communicate with the other adults is rarely covered despite the fact that the relationships with other adults in the school can make or break a teacher who is already under stress in the classroom.

Regular staff meetings have only become the norm relatively recently. The idea of 'supervision' where teachers can talk through what they have been doing is not built into their working life as it is in social work. The new teacher is usually expected to do the same as the experienced one – to be in the classroom most of, if not all, the time. It is no wonder that where there is little support, teachers become defensive when asked about what they are doing and how they are coping. Teachers who find a staffroom where they can freely admit 'I am finding this child difficult' and get support from others can grow in confidence. If they can never express the inevitable feelings of inadequacy and stress which most teachers experience at some time or other then they will never be able to develop or innovate.

Musgrove and Taylor (1969) described the staffroom as 'probably one of the most potent forces for conservatism' in education.

Certainly it can be difficult if the teacher does not conform to the tradition or culture. It takes the bravest teacher to voice a contrary view or challenge the 'received wisdom'. Where staff have seen the importance of working as a group and include team-building in their in-service training the defensiveness begins to disappear. Discussions allow for different attitudes and experiences; staff respect a variety of viewpoints as they move towards a shared vision. Teachers cannot be expected to discuss with parents 'fundamental questions . . . about the family's effects on in-school attainment; about teachers' professional performance and parents' duties' about curriculum and staffing', as Macbeth (1984) has suggested they should, unless they have had the opportunity to think through these ideas as a group.

Being a professional

Even teachers who have always believed in working closely with parents fear that the new powers given to parents could damage their previously good relationships. They worry about the emphasis on parents' 'rights' and the competitiveness among schools as they become involved in market forces. Some believe that the previously established informal home–school links which allowed flexibility with parents are being undermined by the demands for statutory accountability which can place them in opposing positions. And those who have always believed that parents are a nuisance feel even more threatened as the 'troublemakers' become governors. Some teachers complain that parents – egged on by the press and the Secretary of State's constant criticism – believe that they can come in and 'throw their weight around'.

Much of the anxiety stems from the apparent lowering of teachers' status. Since the professionalism of teaching was hard fought for, it has always been closely defended and there is probably more talk about what it constitutes than in any other job. Yet it is not easy to define. Teachers are not self-employed. Unlike lawyers and doctors, they have no single professional body and no control over their training. It is not always clear to whom they are accountable – the Secretary of State, the local authority or the parents. Politically, they have rarely been highly regarded. Aldrich and Leighton (1985) suggest that politicians' concern has generally been for quantity not quality; they have generally seen teachers as 'the servant of the state'. There was no mention of them in the 1944 Education Act. And in the recent Acts, as parents have been given a central place in the educational framework, their autonomy has been removed.

Although a teacher develops skills and knowledge in training, these are not necessarily seen as exclusive to them. A doctor prescribes treatment and gives out medicine which no one else can obtain; a lawyer takes over a case and it becomes his or her brief. It is not always clear where the teacher's job ends and where the responsibility of the parent begins. Both parent and teacher, it seems, are responsible for 'educating' and 'caring' for the children. What should be left to the professional educators and what to the parents is often a source of contention. Everybody has been through school and has some first-hand experience of what it is like: many are prepared to give their opinions about its value and organization and make comparisons between their schooling and what happens today.

The blurring of roles can be difficult for teachers when they feel their training is not appreciated and that their qualifications are not being valued. It is a particular problem for teachers working with the very young children where more and more para-professionals are becoming involved. Yet as Jones *et al.* (1983) point out, having skills which are not just exclusive to them does not mean that they have to defend or abandon their training. Rather it is

an argument for developing training by looking beyond the profession for wisdom and understanding; for being prepared to consider the unorthodox; for learning from parents. . . . Qualifications are important because they represent a standard of professional capacity. If they become merely pieces of paper to be brandished in acquiring a status and a salary, their value will deteriorate.

Involving parents in helping in school is usually seen as an important part of good home–school relations. Yet volunteering – that is, giving your services free – may be regarded as the thin end of the wedge, a way of getting education on the cheap. The National Union of Teachers (1987) has a clear policy that 'work which is properly the task of a paid employee should not be done by a parent or volunteer'. It acknowledges that 'professionalism requires good communication with parents' but is categorical that 'the teacher has a professional role that cannot be fulfilled by non-professionals'. The issue here is where you draw the line. Where does professionalism begin and end? What is parent involvement, what volunteering? Certainly schools would not ask parents to supervise a class when a teacher is away. But how much should a parent help with or introduce her child or her friend's child to mathematical concepts? Should parents hear children read in the classroom and help them over a difficult word? Should a parent bring a guitar in and sing with a group of children?

One union leader suggested that 'children like to play at parents and it seems that many parents like to play at teachers' (Moncur 1985). Teachers have very different views on how much they want parents involved. For some 'just hearing a child read' is acceptable, but actually correcting or introducing a technique is not. As one teacher said, reflecting a view which is commonly expressed: 'I trained for four years to teach reading. I don't see how parents can be expected to do it.'

Undoubtedly the lack of clarity in their role leaves teachers in a vulnerable position. But for some, 'professionalism' seems to be synonymous with status – a status which they feel is being gradually eroded. While one can sympathize with those who feel undermined and unrewarded, their very defensiveness means that they do not explain their role clearly to parents and this then leads to further conflict.

Making judgements

Perceptions of parents are often tinged by attitudes which have permeated educational literature and which, although misinterpreted, stick. There is the notion of the 'good' home. For some teachers, this equates with parents being in agreement with them or bringing their children up in the way they would. Much of this can be traced back to the research in the 1960s when the good home was seen in class terms. It was generally believed that the reason why middle-class children were the main achievers in school was that their parents gave greater encouragement and showed more interest in their education than those from working-class homes. Significantly, research such as that by Douglas (1964) based its definition of parental interest partly on the number of times a parent visited a school and on the teacher's comments about the family. The nature of the school as an institution was not seriously considered. The failure of working-class children appeared to be because parents did not provide, or indeed were not able to provide, the right kind of intellectual framework for the children or prepare them adequately for school. Although Plowden (DES 1967) commented that 'an improvement in school may raise the level of parental interest', the main thrust of the report which was taken up was the need for schools to compensate for the inadequacies of the working-class home.

Words such as 'disadvantage', 'cultural poverty', 'intervention' and 'compensatory' began to abound in the 1960s. Meanings could be value-laden and emotive. The interpretation of 'disadvantage', for instance, depended on the philosophical, psychological and political stance taken. At the extreme it was seen as pathological and perpetuating. Keith Joseph, Secretary of State for Health and Social Services during 1972–3, developed the idea of the 'cycle of deprivation' which could not be easily broken because of parents' inherited inadequacy and poor home background. On the other hand, 'disadvantage' could also be interpreted, as Jackson and Marsden (1962) and Young and McGeeney (1968) argued, as a lack of access to information about the education system. The community education movement was coming to the fore, highlighting the need to take seriously and value children's different cultural experiences and demonstrating the clash of values between home and school.

Nevertheless, the idea of 'disadvantaged' and 'deprived' families is an attitude which still permeates educational thinking. And it is perhaps not surprising that many teachers still hold deficit views of parents. Rarely do more than one or two hands go up at the beginning of an in-service session when people are asked 'How many of you have had any training in working with parents?' 'We had one day on parental involvement' and 'I know we looked at the Plowden Report' are some of the responses. Few teachers had any emphasis put on home–school issues in their initial training. What they have had is often theoretical and out of date, based on the Plowden paradigm of the 'good' home, as Atkin and Bastiani (1985) found in their survey of training colleges.

There is no doubt that some parents are bringing up their children in extremely difficult circumstances. But the 'them and us' syndrome has to be avoided. Parents can feel extremely angry when the area they live in is constantly referred to as 'disadvantaged' and they, by implication, are included. 'What d'you think we feel like', said a parent, 'when we're constantly being put down?' Teachers can recognize 'disadvantage' without being patronizing. In one school, in an area renowned for its terrible housing conditions and lack of facilities, the head saw one of his main tasks as acting as a catalyst to draw attention to them. Damp and crowded homes were affecting children's health and performance. Instead of dwelling on the 'problems', the school was joining with other workers in the neighbourhood to put pressure on the authorities to do something.

They were not responding in a do-gooder, patronizing or critical way.

Judging parents' interest by whether they come into school or not is still common, with the general cry 'But we never see the parents we want to'. But the reasons why parents do not come in are not so often examined. Groups challenged on this will admit that as teachers it is difficult to get to their own children's school, particularly in the daytime when they are working. Pressed even further, some will also admit that as parents they feel uncomfortable at open evenings or – and this is difficult if you are being disloyal to your profession – dissatisfied or unhappy about what is happening to their own children. They recognize that talking to their own children's teachers may mean plucking up courage or overcoming the feeling that you may, after all, just be making a fuss. At one training session, a group of teachers were first asked why they should involve parents: this they found relatively easy. But when asked to put themselves in the role of parents, which most of them were, and say why they as parents might want to be involved, they were reluctant to say. What they were realizing was that their attitudes as teachers were not necessarily compatible with their attitudes as parents.

Frequently, when asked why involve parents, teachers will see it in terms of giving help. They want to help them 'understand what we are trying to achieve', or 'understand more about their own child'. They 'need to know what we're doing and be able to come to us for help and advice'. They 'need to be involved to feel useful and assured that they are a major part of a child's life'. Parents, it appears, have a lot of 'needs'. Teachers are still essentially the givers; they set the boundaries.

Changing relationships

If teachers have had little opportunity to look at why and how they find themselves responding to parents, it is not surprising they feel threatened by the changing relationships. On the one hand, they are being told that the parent has definite rights in the educational system and that teachers should be accountable to them. HMI reports and continuing research claim that parents are essential partners in children's education and that teachers should be finding as many opportunities as possible to involve them more actively. At the same time, some teachers may perceive them as disadvantaged and inadequate.

The majority of teachers have found themselves working perfectly effectively without parents. In primary schools, there is little or no time away from the children and, quite rightly, teachers see them as the focus of their work. Parents would not want this to be different. Nor would they dispute that a child goes to school to learn and be educated. Few primary teachers would believe that learning is purely contextual; indeed, many are concerned that the curriculum laid down is not broad enough. They are trained to build on a child's experience. As children walk into the classroom each day they bring with them a range of experiences; they carry attitudes and expectations learnt from their parents. As most teachers would agree, ignoring and denigrating the learning and development of the children outside means denying them the opportunities to build on these experiences. Thus where teachers put parents down, they put children down, too.

Teachers who use their status to isolate and defend themselves can find themselves in a much more vulnerable position than those who are clear that they are just one of several influential people in a child's life. The demands made by society, families and politicians are not necessarily compatible and what they are sometimes expected to do is impossible. On the one hand, schools are being asked to prepare children for adult life and society. Then they find themselves being blamed for delinquency, poor educational standards and the other ills of society. They can easily become the kicking post. They are asked to support the family, yet education is also seen as a means of social mobility and a way to change the child's environment. While the Plowden Report (DES 1967) emphasized the influence that schools could have, it pointed out that teachers were being asked 'to take on new burdens' which 'will sometimes be next to impossible'. Where teachers recognize parents as part of a child's educational resource then some of these burdens can be lifted.

There is no doubt that the role of the teacher is much more complex than it was even twenty or thirty years ago. But then our whole society is, too. Teachers are part of a web of influences and changes which affect not only themselves but the children they teach. Education is dynamic. Thus the role of the teacher is an evolving one. Those who have taught for many years have gone through the changes. Social conditions, educational theories, the primary school as an institution are very different from when they first started. But the reason for teaching has not changed – the children. That is the starting point for parents and teachers to get together; acknowledging their different responsibilities and recognizing each others' roles is the beginning of parental involvement because it is the beginning of communication.

Although the parent's role has become more central, it is primarily a political one and thus can be seen as threatening and powerful. The parent becomes the customer who 'is always right', a consumer who needs regular reports and to whom teachers are answerable. But are they really the direct consumers? A parent, recognizing that educational methods and content were different from when she was at school, remarked that despite this 'the problems for children are probably much the same – that is, getting on with the teacher and the other children'. Both teachers' and parents' central concern, as a headteacher expressed it, is 'fixed into the good of the child'. That is what they have in common. The difficulty arises when there is disagreement or ignorance of each other's definition of how this should be achieved. And there will be differing views on this among teachers as well as parents. Both need to find out what these are.

CHAPTER 3

Parents – partners or consumers?

'I don't want to be a governor. It's too high for me.'

(Parent)

The responsibility for seeing that children receive full-time education from 5 to 16 lies with parents; it is they who are taken to court if a child does not attend school; it is, as the 1944 Education Act laid down, their 'duty' to see their child 'receive(s) efficient full-time education suitable to his age, ability and aptitude'.

How they have carried out this duty has in the past been limited: parents had few opportunities to influence the type of education their children were receiving and were rarely if ever consulted about the 'efficiency' of it. Although the local education authority was to 'have regard to the general principle that . . . pupils are to be educated in accordance to the wishes of their parents', the Act made it clear that this was to be done where it 'avoided unreasonable public expenditure'.

Some parents have always opted out and educated their children at home, but most children attend school and few parents have felt it their place, or have wanted to challenge publicly, what goes on there. If they have done, they have found themselves not just challenging the school but also a much wider and complicated education system. The 1944 Act was based on the principle of partnership. The partners included central government, local authorities, religious authorities, governing bodies, teachers and parents. They were all supposedly balancing and interacting with each other for a common concern – the children and their education – but they neither necessarily had the same priorities nor indeed always knew about each other's responsibilities.

The very speedy change to a major role for parents in the management of the schools, in the 1986 and 1988 Acts, after the rather vague responsibility as enshrined in the 1944 Act, found most unprepared. Some parents gathered through the press and media that changes were afoot and that teachers were feeling threatened and stressed but few heard the details of what these changes would mean (Lodge 1989b). Teachers worried that they might be being 'forced to do what parents want' and that the national curriculum pandered to the more conservative opinions among them. The increasing parent 'power' enshrined in the Education Acts of the 1980s made them nervous about their position. The political debate, a debate which still rages, hinges on their accountability. All the political parties, and even teachers themselves, have advocated this, but deciding to whom and for what teachers should be accountable has been much more complicated. Whether parents should have to take on that responsibility or indeed are the right people to do so is debatable. A parent governor expressed her concern about having to make sure standards were being reached in the national curriculum. 'I find that difficult', she said, 'because I'm not sure how I could assess and it would be a personal confrontation. I'm not sure that's right. It's the role of the school inspector.'

One of the strongest arguments for teachers and parents to understand each other better has come from research which has shown that where they do work together they can enhance a children's learning. Home reading schemes, for instance, notably in Haringey, Hackney and Rochdale, showed convincingly how children's attainment improves when parents have taken an active part with the teachers (Tizard *et al.* 1981; Griffiths and Hamilton 1984; Jackson and Hannon 1981). Interestingly, this is rarely reported in the popular press, and it is the changing political nature of the education system which attracts the publicity.

Power to parents

There have always been parents interested in extending their rights and in having a greater say in the organization and management of schools. Pressure groups such as the Advisory Centre for Education (ACE) and the Confederation for the Advancement of State Education (CASE) have been campaigning since the 1960s for more information about their children's education and greater involvement.

The shift in the 1980s to more control for central government and less to local authorities led to the change in the parents' political role. As a group they have more rights in law. Where before they had little say on governing bodies, they now have equal representation with those nominated by the local authority. They have been given more choice as to which school their children attend; they can vote for their school to opt out of the local authority. But whether these rights really bring more influence for all parents is a vexed question.

Parents most visibly exercise their rights as governors. They are involved in budgeting and staff appointments and the general management of the school. But only a few choose to take on this role. Although the Minister of Education (BBC 'File on Four', 9 January 1990) argued that greater numbers of parents will become more interested in being part of the political process during the 1990s, past evidence does not suggest this. Most parents are not rushing to put themselves forward as governors. In some areas it is difficult to attract any parents at all, and, although some authorities have made serious attempts to encourage women and people from minority groups, they are still seriously under-represented. Halls in schools are not bursting at the seams as parents flock in for the annual meeting. The Education Acts of the 1980s offered a political process, a mechanism. The legislation came with little detail of how to carry out this process and parent governors found themselves taking on increasingly complex problems.

It is the exercise of this group power which most worries teachers. The idea of parents as managers instead of local authority officers can seem threatening partly because they are not 'professionals' and therefore do not understand their concerns, and also because they are more visible. But although parents have more say, as governors, they learn very quickly how restricted they are by financial constraints and legislation. The main core of education, the curriculum, has not actually been passed to them. It is now primarily in the hands of central government. As governors they discuss it but, unlike groups in the United States, they are not able to demand that certain subjects be taught.

Parents' use of power is often more rhetorical than real. A report in a large local authority in south-west England found that teachers complained not so much about the political pressure from parents but more about their lack of interest and apathy, one head claiming that she was 'under more pressure from central government than parents' (Hughes *et al.* 1990). Research into governing bodies in secondary schools revealed 'little rancour and few flashpoints' and that it was the parent representatives who were particularly suspicious when there seemed to be 'political involvement in deliberations' (Golby 1989). Where parents do take political interest, their allegiance is generally with the school. During the mid-1980s when teachers' industrial action regularly disrupted the schools, the Secretary of State for Education claimed that he had the support of parents. In fact, the main parent groups such as the National Confederation of Parent-Teacher Associations (NCPTA) and CASE, while deploring the disruption to their children's education, publicly supported the teachers in their claim.

Education for sale

The government's introduction of market forces into education during the 1980s has meant that schools and local authorities have had to become increasingly competitive in attracting pupils and funding. When schools are offering packs of stationery and sports insurance and discounts on shower units to any parents enrolling their children (Lodge 1989a), it could appear that parents are now in the marketplace rather than in an education service. Parents as 'consumers' is not a new concept, although its interpretation has differed. Midwinter (1977) called for an approach which made education much more relevant to the community so that it was 'more like everything else' and there was 'a character of normalcy' in home–school relations. Being 'for sale' meant that education was more available, less elitist and accessible to everyone. It was very different from the idea of consumerism in the 1980s, which took on an individualistic and competitive connotation.

It is where parents demand an education for their children which runs counter to the values or objectives of the school, or indeed society, that conflict arises. Accountability is different from being answerable to the individual and possibly idiosyncratic demands of every parent. When an education authority has a policy of equal opportunities, for instance, should it allow parents to take a child away from the school and go to another one in the same authority because they do not like their children in a school which celebrates other religious festivals in addition to Christmas? This happens, and it is a question of where choice conflicts with other people's rights or what responsibility society has for individuals.

The vagueness of the legislation can often work in favour of a minority of parents. Although the 1988 Education Reform Act has given parents much more choice about which school their children attend, this is still dependent on the availability of places and the appeals system would still put many parents off. Even more important, it also depends on the mobility of families and their ease of access to information. As schools publish results, parents will be able to make comparisons. This is nothing new; they have always discussed whether their children's school is as good as the others in the area and whether it compares with their friends' or relations' children's schooling. What is different now is that the information is public. It is not just hearsay or rumour. If parents are to make judgements and decisions then how this information is transmitted and com-municated, what it is, and who receives it will be vital. It needs to be accurate and relevant.

Whenever schools find themselves in competition with each other, so will parents as they try to get the 'best' for their children at the expense of others. The irony is that although it is now widely accepted that involving parents in their children's learning can decrease the differentials between middle-class and working-class achievement, the legislation giving parents' increased powers could still inhibit their chances. If parents are 'well-informed, articulate, persistent and listened to' then, as Wragg (1989) suggests, they could be highly influential; but 'the distribution of these necessary circum-stances and characteristics is by no means even'. 'Public expenditure' still remains an issue in whether children are educated in 'accordance to the wishes' of their parents. As private funding becomes an increasingly important part of the education system, those in the better-off schools still continue to benefit the most.

Who cares about the children?

Parents are quite naturally mainly concerned about what is happen-ing to their own children. Most teachers recognize this and, indeed, the focus on the individual child has always been at the heart of the primary school ethos. Discussions between teachers and parents about children's achievement have been formalized. But as the Hargreaves Report (ILEA 1985) emphasized, if all parents are to be involved and if parents and teachers are truly going to work together then there is the need for partnership as well as power. The idea of 'becoming partners in a shared task for the benefit of the child' (DES 1985b) is one to which many teachers and parents have always aspired. But the enormous imbalance between the 'partners' is often overlooked. Partnership implies equality and with this needs to come empowerment. Empowerment is different from having powers thrust upon one. Although parents seem to be getting power, it may not be the kind that they want. What it amounts to is also clearly dependent on who and where they are. O'Hagan (1986) has described empowerment in community education as 'providing people with knowledge and skills which allow them to struggle for and gain power for themselves'. Fletcher (1989) contrasts this 'direction and achievement of critical democracy' with the fact that the Secretary of State 'is empowered' over 450 times in the Education Reform Act. Empowerment is a process; fundamental changes are needed in attitudes and policy if all parents and teachers are going to be able to work in a partnership where each has equal rights, where there is the opportunity to express these and where they work first and foremost for the benefit of the children. It is often forgotten that the children are the direct consumers; they need to be at the heart of any debate.

During the last few years where teachers have been asked, on the one hand, to draw closer to parents in partnership for the good of the child and, at the same time, have felt threatened by the rhetoric of parents' rights and calls for accountability, it is no wonder that many have become cynical. They complain that parents 'just aren't interested' and want to shed their responsibility. Or they ask too many questions and implicitly criticize their competence. Yet several studies (Becher *et al*. 1981; Elliott *et al*. 1981) have shown that parents are wanting to trust teachers' skills and competence. Their interest is not in the content and organization of the classroom: this they see as the teacher's concern. Thus general meetings about the curriculum, organized by teachers, as Munn (1988) found, are generally poorly attended, and this can be interpreted as a lack of interest in school. When the focus is on individual children and direct parent–teacher communication, however, then attendance is much higher. What is important to note about this research is 'that parents wanted more information about their children's progress at school as a way of helping them through school, not as a means of monitoring teacher competence. Parents did not generally have doubts about this competence.'

Where teachers value the parents' knowledge and experience of the child and acknowledge that they are one of many educators in the child's life, then they begin to see parents as partners. Parents' highly emotional interest in their own children becomes a strength; they will support the person who supports their child. They will begin to understand the reality of the task, not hark back to the mythical teachers who gave their all to the children and changed the world at the same time.

PART II

What happens in practice?

In talking to teachers and parents about their theories, practices, constraints and anxieties, I have tried to come closer to knowing how the rhetoric of parent partnership can be translated into reality. The most important question is not so much what it looks like but what possibilities open up when teachers and parents begin to understand each other and so together begin to support and educate the child.

Most of the examples in Part II come from heads, teachers and parents whom I interviewed in three education authorities for a small research project on the meaning of parent–teacher partnership. The questions raised with them came under the following broad headings:

- Why do you believe it is important to involve parents and encourage parent–teacher partnership?
- What steps are taken to involve parents more fully?
- Who actually gets involved?
- What will partnership mean for teachers and parents?

CHAPTER 4

Into school

'A lot of people start trying to involve parents and then wonder why it doesn't happen'.

(Headteacher)

It is clear that there is no single formula for involving parents. What happens in one school may not be appropriate for another. Much of what evolves is either because of particular circumstances or personnel with special skills and interests and it takes time to build up relationships. Nevertheless, there are components common to schools where parents and teachers work closely together; there are reasons why what works in one school does not in another.

Most schools accept, and have put into practice, Plowden's guidelines for distributing information and making parents welcome. Parent-teacher associations, open evenings and regular letters home are commonplace. Yet it is possible to do all that Plowden suggests – which was, after all, a minimum requirement – and still have very little contact with parents. Even where one school puts on more activities than another the relations between parents and teachers may be more open and honest in the one where little ostensibly seems to be happening.

By controlling information and initiating any dialogue or activities on their own terms, teachers can keep a safe distance and avoid any possible disagreements. They do not necessarily do this consciously but, as Tizard *et al.* (1981) pointed out, 'teachers are often uneasily aware that parents' reasons for advocating increased involvement may differ from their own'. Like the headteacher who admits that when someone makes a suggestion he does not like he only has to say 'I don't think that's a good idea, do you?' for the idea to be dropped, teachers can use their 'authority' to anticipate any controversy.

Parental involvement, then, need be no more than an acknowledgement that parents should be given information. On the other hand, it can become a central part of policy, with parents having an active and important influence on the school. There are two extreme approaches. The totally 'school-based' one judges parents only in terms of their role with the school. They are designated someone's 'mum' or 'dad', expected to turn up when asked, to respond to information that is sent to them and to conform to the school's norms. This is a passive role for parents. At the other end of the spectrum are schools where there is a more open or 'community-based' approach. Teachers recognize that parents are members of a wider group and acknowledge that they have other significant roles and skills. They are aware of influences in the community which are outside the school's control. Rather than defending themselves against these, they will face up to or appreciate them, at the same time, being clear about what they have to offer. Parenting becomes a valued and active role.

Some parents will themselves see their role as a passive one. They expect teachers to get on with the job, not ask for their opinions. They may be surprised when asked in to help if they have been brought up in a tradition where parents were never invited to participate. Their previous concept of the authoritarian teacher may be challenged. This means they may be uncertain of what is expected. This can get in the way of becoming actively involved even where schools are encouraging them.

Involving parents is a developmental process and as teachers become more analytical about the way they are engaged with parents they are able to see more clearly where their school is. Sometimes parents will be involved in one or several ways and actually come in; others will seemingly be always outside so using activities as a scale of measurement for involvement is simplistic. More important, as the examples below illustrate, is to look at the underlying attitudes of parents and teachers and how these affect the outcome of the relationship between them and the children.

Parents as supporters

Social events are usually an important part of the school life. Headteachers may feel that these are good opportunities for parents from different social and cultural groups to come together and to be part of the school community. They can be successful in attracting those who might not turn up to other events. Schools are sometimes the only social facility in the area and parties, concerts and festivals enable families to get together.

Even when there is a good turnout, schools' approach to these events can vary considerably. In a school-based model, the events are always organized by the teachers or a selected group of parents. The role for most parents is a passive one. It may be argued, and often is, that this is how they want it to be. And certainly the input by staff may have to be greater in some schools than others or indeed, during particular periods of development, when, for instance, an event is taking place for the first time. But when teachers complain 'they're not interested; they won't do anything for themselves' or 'it's always the same ones who volunteer or want to be involved', then it is time to ask questions. It may be true that parents do not have the energy or time to help. They may also be receiving other messages. For if the teachers and small band of helping parents resent putting on these events or if the main motive is to be seen 'involving parents' then what is this saying? This school is an open and friendly place but only by our invitation, at certain times of day and for certain people?

When a social event takes place in a school with a 'community' approach, the role for parents takes on a more vital aspect. If parents do not want to take an active part at first then that is acceptable. The chances are, as many schools have found, that some who appear to be disinterested or unforthcoming may later get involved. Not everyone wants to be an organizer but when they wish to be they get the opportunity, support or encouragement. Some parents will not have as much energy as others, and there are usually good reasons for this; some will just enjoy taking a more active part than others. But there is no elitism; everyone is part of the same school community. 'Supporters', like football fans, are very varied, but what they have in common is that they all cheer on and want success for the home team – their children's school.

Most schools organize fund-raising events – indeed, for many schools, they are essential. Again, what happens depends on the confidence of the staff with parents. Sometimes the money goes into a general fund for equipment or is spent on social events, presents and treats for the children. Some teachers are concerned that parents may disagree on how the money is spent. Yet it is likely that when parents are not told, they will be together in the playground speculating. One headteacher was worried that parents were being asked to contribute more and more to essential equipment and that they might complain about this. Schools where these kinds of issue are discussed usually find a considerable amount of support. In one school, the headteacher arranged with the PTA that a third of its takings would be used to supplement school holiday fees. So that the children and parents were in no way stigmatized, she agreed with the PTA that they were not told who would be subsidized; because they were involved in the decision-making and understood the reason there was complete acceptance that some parents had greater needs than others.

The celebration of different religious and cultural festivals is also common in most schools. Many teachers see these as a way of giving recognition to the children's different backgrounds, and an opportunity to involve parents as well. The way these events happen needs to be carefully thought out. Parents are quick to pick up token gestures or lip-service to ideas. A headteacher experiencing the failure of a Diwali play and celebration recognized afterwards that not enough preparation with parents had gone into it. Nervousness about the reaction from a section of them meant that she did not explain its context; it had turned out to be a divisive rather than integral and positive event so that no one was satisfied.

Celebrations can become meaningless if they are imposed rather than introduced as an extension of the children's and parents' experience. As a headteacher in a multicultural area (Mulvaney 1984), writes:

There are enormous spin-offs from this hierarchical form of culturalism. The minority parents turn out to provide food, costumes, artefacts, etc. and appear to be eternally grateful. At the end of all such events staff and parents say 'namaste' to each other, and the school reverts to its celebration of white, male, middle class experience. The parents return to their own experience.

Parents as learners

Giving parents information about what their children are learning and doing is a central concern for schools. Again the way this is done will have a profound effect on the outcome. In the 'school-based approach teachers may well organize curriculum workshops and invite parents into the classroom. But it is on their terms. Questions and discussions are not encouraged. The teachers are the experts giving advice; they point out the child's developmental progress and may show parents how to play useful educational games. But they do not ask for or consider valuable the reciprocal information about the child at home.

Where teachers recognize that parents have a life outside school and experience which is different then a dynamic, two-way approach – that is, a community-based approach – can be developed. Parents will bring their own experiences of learning and have opportunities to see this in relation to their children's learning process. The dialogue becomes mutually revealing, leading to what Midwinter (1977) calls 'educational understanding of the parents and the social understanding of the teacher'.

Teachers can be disappointed and aggrieved when they put a great deal of effort into disseminating information and then get little response. Curriculum workshops, for instance, sometimes seem only to attract those parents who are regular visitors anyway. A school where the staff had worked hard to put on an evening display of maths equipment and methods of working felt naturally reluctant to do anything similar again when it did not seem to be appreciated. There were, in fact, several reasons why this may not have worked – reasons which can be looked at before an event is put on. It may have been because the school was on an estate where people did not like coming out, where there were many single parents and couples with very young children. Or it may have been that this was not an appropriate event at this stage and staff needed to look at other ways of encouraging parents to come in. What works in one school does not necessarily in another. Perhaps most importantly, it may have been because the parents were not interested in this kind of event – nobody had asked them if this was what they wanted.

One school which was just beginning to open its doors to parents combined an exhibition of basic curriculum work, by children in all the classes, with an open week, when members of the community could come in at any time of the day. The headteacher felt that this would not only be an opportunity for parents to come and see what was happening – something which they had had few chances of doing before – but that it would also help staff. Although it was a disruption to the normal routine the exhibition led to staff discussions and in-service training and a greater mutuality between teachers as they worked for the first time on a whole-school project. They also got positive feedback from parents and others in the community. Another minor point, worth noting, was that they did not have to get into the numbers game, worrying how many would turn up on the night. Parents came when it was convenient for them and they not only saw examples of their children's work but saw them in action, too.

In another school, the parent-teacher association had shed its responsibility for fund-raising and was only concerned with curriculum. It arranged a computer day, maths and science evening, a session to introduce paired reading, and reading workshops. The meetings were arranged around the parents' concerns; they asked the questions. By being involved in the organization, they also incidentally learnt a good deal about the structure of the education service. They invited advisers in and heard about in-service training for teachers, so were aware that it was not just another day off for them when the school closed. This was not a school where parents were practised in ringing up officials or organizing meetings but by developing into this kind of PTA it gave several an opportunity to develop skills in doing this and many barriers were broken down.

Clearly some teachers are more at ease or confident to be with parents than others and the way meetings and groups develop will often be dependent on the teachers' outlook. Some find themselves taking control to avoid conflict or what they consider irrelevances. One headteacher said that he had stopped the proceedings of a parents' forum because questions had become personal or critical. He had changed the format so that questions were submitted in advance in writing and had to be 'relevant', not just focusing on individual children's problems.

Group discussions are notoriously difficult when people are not sure why they are there or what questions are 'allowed'. Workshops, arranged by the staff at the end of a school day, were particularly successful mainly because they took place regularly and concentrated on a topic for several weeks. Teachers and parents were both more confident when they had something specific to talk about, and having several meetings meant that everyone gradually grew more at ease. There was time to get to know each other and actually discuss issues together. A workshop on reading had focused on the different teaching methods used and had engendered many questions. Parents whose first language was phonically based were surprised that the children were not learning phonic methods as they had done. Teachers had not taken this into account but were able to explain what parents wanted to know rather than what they thought they should know. The parents had gone on to ask to see reference books and guidelines which teachers used and the head felt that many misunderstandings had been sorted out and questions asked which parents would not previously have considered raising for fear of being thought ignorant. Instead of feeling that parents were criticizing, teachers began to realize that it was genuine interest.

Discussing the educational purpose of the school is vital where people's own experience may have been very different. Yet there are still teachers who take the attitude that because parents do not speak English they do not understand anything at all or are probably not interested. The schools who do take communicating with parents seriously find that there are often only limited services which can help with translating and interpreting. Since there is a national shortage of teachers from minority groups only a few schools have staff who are bilingual. They, along with parents who give their services voluntarily, can find themselves being stretched to the limit. Yet it is important to arrange groups with translators or organize meetings in languages other than English. There is also an obvious need for more one-to-one contact, outreach work and use of community group networks but since such schemes are generally funded from outside they can find themselves in a peripheral position. Even where teachers are appointed to do outreach work they can find themselves set apart and cast in the role of troubleshooter unless there is a whole-school policy to improve the communication between all teachers and minority parents. As Tomlinson (1984) has stressed, minority parents of every social class have high expectations of education for their children. If they are not given the opportunity to learn about what is going on this can only lead to suspicion and a lack of interest in what the school is offering.

Parents as helpers

Ask teachers whether parents are involved in their school and they will often reply 'well there are only about five who come in regularly'. For many 'helping in the classroom' seems to be the outward, visible sign that parents really are involved. Yet there is tension here if the activity is not really thought out. Teachers complain that parents 'don't seem to realize that they have to clear up', that 'they favour their own children'. Parents on the other hand, complain that they 'don't know what to do', 'find some of the children difficult' or 'don't like to say they could do more'.

In a purely school-based approach, only certain parents who are deemed suitable are invited to carry out designated tasks. Where schools have the community approach, not only do helpers come into school but teachers also recognize that they may be actively or potentially active outside and that this has an affect on the children as well. They may be involved with other parents in adult education or community groups; they may be organizing or helping in neighbourhood groups or preschool and after-school services. Schools will be aware of these groups, either because they use the school premises or because their activities are linked closely with the educational life of the children, like, for instance, the local playgroups or mosque; they value them as part of the community to which they themselves belong. Doing things for the school is not the only means of helping children.

If involvement is judged on the visibility of the parents in the school then teachers will feel that they are not being successful when they are not there. In reality, most schools only have a handful of parents who regularly help in the classroom. There are those who never come because they work or want a break from their children. It is, after all, not everyone's vocation to work with groups of children. A few respond to general invitations included in the school booklet or on the notice board but generally they come because of a specific invitation or persuasion. In one school a form went out to all parents asking for their help and giving them a list of activities to volunteer for. Obviously not all parents replied, but it seemed a wasted opportunity when the headteacher felt that he could not use all those that did; he felt he needed an organizer to arrange appropriate jobs for them. In another school, waiting for offers, a parent said rather wistfully, 'I'd like to help, but I'm still waiting to be asked' – a view also reflected by others.

The appropriateness of parents' help concerns many teachers. Some believe that the classroom is not always the right place for them; they might have a child who would be unsettled by their presence or accompanying toddlers who are disruptive. The extent of the help also depends on teachers' views; many have strong reservations about the kind of things that parents should be asked to do. As well as the obvious safety factors, there are jobs which they consider should remain with them. Generally teachers believe that basic subjects are their province and they express anxieties about standards and confidentiality. There may also be tension between parents and the paid helpers in school, who have frequently been parents in the school themselves. Unless their role is clear parents may wonder why they get paid to do the jobs which they could 'just as easily do'. The helpers equally need to be aware of the policy of inviting parents in or they can feel threatened or resentful.

In several schools, parents are invited in to tell stories – especially in their mother-tongue – or listen to children read. Sometimes they cook or sew with children in small groups. How much they do will generally depend on the teacher. Things can go badly wrong when teachers have not really thought out the implications of having another adult in the classroom. What emerges from many parents is that they want to know what their role is; they need some direction. That is, they need to know why they are being asked in and what sort of help is wanted, otherwise they can feel 'like a spare leg'. One mother stopped helping in school because she felt she had become a 'dogsbody' and preferred to spend the time cleaning her own home rather than the classroom! She had come, she thought, to help with the children's activities and believed she had much to offer in this area which was not being taken into account.

In a few schools teachers ask parents in who they consider are 'lonely', 'depressed' or 'worried about their child'. But on the whole, it seems that teachers prefer to invite those they can 'rely on'; they do not feel they have time to work with parents who are not able to 'just get on with it'. Those who do invest time in preparation and consultation usually find it pays off and stops much of the frustration and irritation as well as proving much more beneficial for the children. A conscious check of who is actually helping in the school needs to be made regularly. Schools can find that divisions emerge. Some teachers discovered that it was mainly white parents who were offering their services and had therefore made sure that black parents were equally welcomed not only by them but by the other parents, too.

In some schools with a great social mix, there is a division between middle-class and working-class parents in the kind of help they offer. One school found that the middle-class parents preferred to offer a particular skill, often professional, such as pottery, dancing or music: the working-class parents either offered or were generally asked for servicing help. When they became aware of what was happening they encouraged the working-class group to do other things – eventually this group found the confidence to write and put on a play for the children.

Some schools see the help parents give as an adult learning opportunity as well as being of benefit to the children. A school where parents were not confident about giving help tried out a scheme where tasks with the children were clearly defined. They awarded 'certificates' mainly because this gave incentive to one particular mother who spent a lot of time in school but did not seem to know what to do. When cooking, for instance, parents were asked to prepare the children for the activity, cook something which involved their active participation, talk to the children and supervise the clearing up afterwards. An art certificate for which parents were asked to work on six different art or craft ideas was also introduced. The teachers were not suggesting that this idea was a definitive way of including parents in the classroom; they realized it would not be appropriate for many parents. But it had worked for several who had felt inadequate but were very much wanting to give some help. What it also illustrated was the importance of giving parents a clear focus of what is expected and opportunities to develop their skills of working with groups. Many teachers seem to forget that working with other people's children is a new experience for some parents and is very different from working with one's own.

Having another adult in the class should be a positive asset. But people are often put off by the initial difficulties and need for changes. Parents will come in with preconceived ideas about what teachers should be like, usually based on their past experience. They may not like to show initiative, particularly if they believe, as a parent expressed it, that 'teachers like to rule the roost and, as nice as they are and well intentioned, I do feel they like to be solely in charge.' There is learning on both sides and, as Redfern found, 'it took me a long time as a teacher to trust children to be responsible for their own learning, and even longer to realize that trusting parents to do a good job worked every bit as well' (Edwards and Redfern 1988). One education liaison officer succinctly put it thus: 'You can involve parents for their enlightenment. But you shouldn't involve them so it demeans people.'

Parents as teachers

The gap between parents 'helping' and 'teaching' can be a narrow one. Although many schools invite parents in to help, allowing parents to take initiative or responsibility and have a more overtly educative role is contentious. Many teachers believe that parents should not be expected to 'teach' children in school, either because it undermines their special skills and professional training or because other parents may object. There are considerable differences among teachers about what 'teaching' implies; taking a small group for cooking or sewing is fairly common practice; 'just hearing children read' is acceptable, but actually correcting them or introducing a new technique is not.

An increasing number of teachers are beginning to appreciate parents' unique relationship with their children and their continuous role in their child's development. They see that they are not the sole 'educators' and that children's other experiences are important. Those teachers who start to work directly with parents in the education of the children find that it leads to more understanding and therefore more support from parents for the learning processes which go on in school. Where teachers have a more 'school-based' approach the role of the parent as an educator is either not acknowledged or not valued. When they ask parents to carry out tasks with their children they ask them to follow certain rules and not to step into the teacher's territory. Work carried out at home becomes 'homework' rather than an attempt to continue the learning experience in the home.

It is mainly in reading that teachers are exploring ways to work more closely with parents. Where home reading schemes have been introduced, they have clearly demonstrated to teachers the interest that parents have in being involved educatively with their children. Several who were not entirely convinced before have changed their minds because they have provided a solid base from which to start with parents and have been part of an overall policy to involve parents more fully in other aspects of their children's learning. It gives teachers an opportunity to keep in touch with parents whom they might not normally meet. There is an element of accountability on both sides as teachers provide appropriate material and share information and parents report back to the teacher about what the child has achieved. Nevertheless, there is also an inherent danger if teachers merely see this link with parents in terms of a useful 'scheme'. The nature of the commitment between teacher and parent is crucial. By asking parents to hear their children read at home, teachers are affirming them as a valuable resource, not just a teacher's aide.

Although the learning takes place at home, teachers will still have to confront their professionalism, as they do when parents are asked into school. They will have to decide how much information they will share and be clear about the role of the parent as a 'teacher' of the child. Teachers cannot expect parents to take up a purely passive role at home as they carry out the instructions. Genuinely involving parents may mean teachers giving up their prerogative over special teaching methods and sharing information which they have felt was part of their professionalism. It may mean giving parents opportunities to extend their knowledge, through meetings, discussions and workshops, of how children learn. It will certainly result in parents asking more questions and wanting more answers.

Parents as policy-makers

The main place for parents as policy-makers is as governors, although this actually accounts for very few. Their voices can certainly be heard if they wish to raise them, but even in this position of apparent 'power', parents can find themselves taking on a relatively passive role. It is easy to accept 'the appropriate roles and duties within the school system' (Bacon 1978) particularly where there is a lack of training opportunities or people are new to the position. Many are overwhelmed by the responsibility they have to take on and can feel extremely inadequate as they wrestle with new legislation and policies.

A school with a community approach will understand how the power structures can inhibit people from participating or expressing their views. They realize that since governors give their services voluntarily it will only attract some people. Many parents have neither the time nor the desire to attend meetings. Although parents were given a 'greater say in the running of their children's schools' by the 1986 Education Act, to interpret this as massive powers is to exaggerate; they have equal representation with the local education authority governors. In schools where these representatives are parents as well, teachers often find they have increased support as they really know what is happening in school. And as one parent expressed it, 'you're there to help and support not to make more problems'. Several heads stress the advantages of being appointed by governors knowing that one has their support. Likewise parent governors see this as part of their role and feel that if they are on an interview panel then they have a real responsibility to appoint the best people for the school.

Certainly there are times when parent governors can be difficult. But they, too, can find themselves in an awkward position; they soon learn that being a governor requires more than a special interest in one's own child, particularly when this goes against the main consensus of opinion. People need to be aware of what the role involves because to be effective one needs time to follow educational theory and practice, visit the school and understand the practice of management. It is, as several governors find to their cost, not a matter of 'just using one's authority, but hard work'. It is not surprising that several schools find it difficult to attract 'just ordinary people'.

Yet policy affects all parents. Parent governors are expected to take an active role in drawing others in. There is an annual meeting where governing bodies have to present a report to other parents. But these meetings, like curriculum ones, are often not well attended. Schools therefore find themselves needing to disseminate information in a variety of ways. What is important is that the aims and objectives are discussed openly and that policy is not just seen as belonging to a few governors.

Parent-teacher associations can also have a 'powerful' position in the school, although several complain that there are only a few who take a really active part. The role of the PTA is frequently dependent on the headteacher and whether teachers are involved or not. Some are concerned purely with social events and fund-raising and there is a danger, particularly with the need for extra money, that some will find themselves only having time to do this. Yet PTAs who have moved on to look at other issues have found it a useful place to ask questions and give their opinions.

The notion of parents as policy-makers is new for schools, and with present structures not easy to put into practice. Unless they have information it is not easy to take an active constructive part. This applies to governors as well as individual parents. Finding different forums which allow not just the few and articulate to express their opinions is important if 'ordinary' people are going to feel happy to come forward into the more formal ones. As one parent said, 'I never thought I'd land up being chair of the PTA – maybe I'll be a governor one day!'

CHAPTER 5

Fitting into the organization

'I always feel there should be more questions that I should ask but I can never really think of the questions to ask. I don't know why.'

(Parent)

The amount and style of teacher–parent contact will depend a great deal on attitudes. But the school as an organization can also inhibit development and in urging teachers to work more closely with parents this cannot be ignored. Even newly built schools generally have the look of an institution – an institution which all adults have their own good or bad memories of. Making them look and feel friendly or inviting takes time and effort.

An 'open door' policy

Schools may have 'open door' policies, but many schools were not built for easy, informal access: they date back from the days when boys and girls were segregated so that there were several entrances and children left their parents behind once they entered the school's gate. Some parents remember, and indeed believe, that the teachers have the responsibility for the children during school time and do not see school as a place for them as well. Primary school teachers have little time scheduled to be outside the classroom and, unless given the responsibility for home–school liaison, neither see this as part of their timetable nor feel that contacts with parents can take precedence over their work with the children.

Welcome signs and notices certainly help. Yet even then there are other difficulties that sometimes have to be surmounted. A head-teacher at an infant school with no ground floor and concrete steps leading up to the classroom wanted to reverse the previous tradition of excluding parents from school. Overcoming the staff's arguments, she wrote to parents inviting them to collect their children from the classrooms. She almost abandoned the idea on the first day when a toddler had an accident on the stairs. But despite the staff's 'told you so' looks she continued until parents were used to the dangers and began to take responsibility themselves for seeing children went up and down carefully.

Even meeting their children at the end of the day can be an unpleasant experience for parents who are isolated or shy. Coming into the school is not the problem but being with the other parents is. It is important to be aware of the cliques that form, as one headteacher found when she realized that the less assured were standing in the rain as others talked loudly in the hall. Groups like this can become a strong influence in decision-making as their voices are the ones that are heard. The claim 'parents want this', when analysed, may turn out to come from only four or five of the more vociferous parents.

Parents in some areas where there have been attacks in the neighbourhood or threatening graffiti on the walls may also be wary of coming to the school and even find it an ordeal. Teachers know of the harassment that some of their families receive. Some go out of their way to help them; at one school, for example, teachers took it in turns to escort a family who had suffered an arson attack to and from their home. There may be complaints that parents are too lazy to walk to school but, as one parent pointed out, although living nearby, she always arranged to have her children collected by car because she was afraid of walking the streets. Teachers in many schools now understand the difficulty of having late afternoon or evening meetings, especially in the winter, because of parents' fears of walking in the dark. At a meeting I attended in London one evening, I asked how many women had walked or come on public transport; the answer was none. People had arranged lifts with each other or had brought cars; no one lived more than a mile and a half (2.5 km) away. It is easy to forget, as a teacher, what it feels like walking in the dusk alone with small children and perhaps unable to speak English.

Teachers who recognize that some people may be nervous about coming into schools will try to put them at their ease. The classroom or headteacher's room is not always the best place for discussions. There is often a need for a 'neutral' room; as one teacher put it, 'you both have to feel comfortable to discuss issues you may not agree on'. Privacy is important, too; some headteachers still share their rooms with the secretary, so she either remains in the background, which can inhibit the conversation – especially as she may be a parent too – or has to be asked to leave when someone comes in, which makes the interview seem more formal.

Asking parents to use the school as a resource for themselves also requires thought and planning. Having a space for them in school is generally dependent on the headteacher's sense of priority. Parents' rooms are becoming more common, especially in infant schools. But they can still be a cause of concern in the organization of the school. Who uses them? When? Where should they be located? These are all questions that have to be sorted out. The room may, as a headteacher suggested, 'look a dump but then no one worries about their small children making a mess' and, as she emphasized, 'they can feel relaxed'.

The kind of space given to parents, community teachers, home visitors or other 'extra' people in the school can reveal a lot about the kind of status they have. Being allocated a space to work with parent groups a long way from the main part of the school and not easily accessible, can represent graphically to community teachers how most of the staff see them. Parents' rooms need to be in a suitable place and easy to enter. Usually, when a teacher decides to start a group, rooms already being used have to be rearranged or adapted, and this may not be popular with other members of staff. A new headteacher who had to move an aggrieved teacher to another room so that parents and toddlers had easy access to toilets had to deal with the consequences; as he realized, this did not help nurture good relations among staff let alone between parents and teachers; although he had several grateful parents he also had one very resentful teacher.

Even where there are 'ideal' conditions, it is still possible for teachers to avoid real contact with the parents. Having a designated room does not necessarily mean it is a meeting place for teachers *and* parents. Some teachers never go in. Even where schools have community centres it does not follow that the teachers use them nor that parents go more easily to the classrooms. Community resources sometimes mean little more than shared accommodation and, as one teacher cynically commented: 'some teachers believe that community education happens at night with somebody else.'

Whatever the condition, it will in the end be the personal response which will hinder or help the growth of good parent–teacher relations. Teachers can stand at the door or put up lots of welcoming notices in different languages, but, as one bilingual parent said – reflecting a view also expressed in the Thomas Report (ILEA 1985) –

'when people are friendly, you don't need to speak the same language. You can understand a lot.'

Outside the classroom

Almost without exception, most people, whether they be teachers, advisers or parents, put the responsibility for the ethos of the school, and the relations within it, on headteachers. With the increasing demand on them as managers and the complexity of the job, knowing where their role begins and ends can bring tensions and stress. Many headteachers highlight the 'unrealistic' and 'tremendous' expectations that both teachers and parents have of them as well as the pressures put on them by central government, governors and the local authority.

Although most are now appointed as non-teaching heads, how much time they give to parents can prove a difficult decision. And what develops often depends on their personal interests. Many are concerned by the increasing number of outside commitments that take them away from the children. They also need to find time for teachers who are developing projects or in-service training. When there are few staff or frequent absences they may have to take on a large teaching commitment.

Several heads complain that teachers still see it as an easy option to sit talking to parents. And one problem is distinguishing between parents genuinely needing time or help which is appropriate for headteachers to give and those who either 'take too much time', become dependent or need a service which the school cannot provide. One head put it: 'I don't know where I draw the line. You have to weigh up each individual case.'

The dependence on one person for 'good' parental involvement can lead to conflict and frustration. Although the main thrust for improved home–school relations certainly has to come from the head, to expect these to be achieved by one person alone is unrealistic. It demands a whole school policy which will affect not only the structure and organization but also the way staff work and their expectations of each other.

The advent of the national curriculum has brought more opportunities for staff to discuss educational issues, teaching methods and content. But democratic argument can still be hard for staff who have not been used to putting forward their point of view or who have found that any disagreements in the past have led to increased tension in the staffroom. Newly appointed heads who are keen to change the structure so that it is easier for parents to approach teachers can find themselves extremely unpopular. One who wanted to open the school, so that parents could be involved in discussions and group activities denied them before, was distressed by how hard it was to change staff attitudes. 'The problem is,' he said, 'I want to be democratic about the school organization, but I find I have to be autocratic with staff . . . There are opportunities for staff to transfer to other schools or go on courses, but it's not happening.'

This uneasy dual role of democrat and autocrat is exemplified by another, more established, head. On arriving at the school she quite categorically stated her intention to involve the community in the school. If staff did not like this, she would, she said, support them if they wanted to apply for other jobs. After a while she had a team of teachers who agreed with her policy.

Not many headteachers find it easy to take this kind of stand or to demand that teachers involve parents. Teachers' central concern, quite naturally and properly, is the children. Yet since involving parents is becoming a more accepted part of teachers' work it is essential that schools develop clear policies and priorities. Since the 1970s, there have been an increasing number of staff in primary schools with non-teaching roles, yet the assumption still remains that teachers are not really doing a 'proper' job unless they are in front of a class of children. Teachers who have little time away from the children are not always sympathetic to those who do not rush out of the staffroom immediately the bell goes and who appear to have an easy life drifting about the neighbourhood and visiting parents at home.

Those teachers with specific home–school liaison or community posts often express feelings of frustration and isolation because their job is seen as extracurricular. Community teachers with a home-visiting brief or room separate from the school speak of the 'out of sight, out of mind' attitude that they meet. They find themselves cast as the one who 'deals with parents'. They can also feel vulnerable where there are teacher shortages. 'Drinking cups of tea' with parents may be regarded as an easy way out of the classroom. Having a teacher in school whose only responsibility is to work with parents is a perk but not when other teachers have to double up classes because someone is away. To withstand these pressures they need plenty of support and a clear understanding of their role.

One community teacher was particularly frustrated at the way she was cast as the 'expert' with parents. She considered that one of her main tasks was to work with the staff and parents together and not act as a go-between. Another in a school where staff had actually demonstrated their commitment to home–school developments by opting for an extra post to be used for this, was also concerned by the lack of understanding. Since she had special teaching abilities which she was able to put to use in the school, she had credibility with staff. But 'sitting in the parents' room' was not seen as work, and although teachers accepted support from her in the classroom, they generally preferred that she made the initial contact with parents.

Teachers who want to work much more closely with parents and encourage communication are constantly frustrated by their lack of time or by finding they are a lone voice in the staffroom. Although there is now a formal commitment to see parents regularly, the informal contacts are still valued and seen as extremely important by parents and teachers alike. Yet parents may find that one year they have easy access to the class teacher and the next year none at all. This difference in attitudes was summed up by a teacher who said: 'There are two of us who leave our classroom doors open and encourage parents to see us at the beginning and end of the day – the rest keep their doors firmly closed.'

What sort of organization?

In opening up a school to take account of parents and children, there are many dilemmas to face and questions to be asked in the way things are organized. Priorities change and mistakes are made. Yet these, in my experience, and as Edwards and Redfern (1988) found, 'can be forgiven in an atmosphere in which parents and teachers respect one another, where there is a genuine will to try and do better and accommodate everybody's needs and interests.' Just because the links between parents and teachers are informal, it does not follow that there needs to be vagueness in the overall policy about parental involvement.

The needs of parents and children will differ greatly not only among, but also within, schools and this will affect the role the school takes on in the community. Headteachers whom I inter- viewed gave varied reasons for opening up the school. Some saw the school as a resource, as 'a meeting place for the community'. One head emphasized the lack of facilities in the area and the need to use the school to develop these. An infant school head felt the school should be an extension of the home; several others saw it as an integral part of the community. It could be a 'logical place for helping the community' and it was even described as an 'educational

corner shop'. Some heads stressed the pressure that many parents
were under and believed that schools should 'make life a bit easier'
where the environment could 'cheer them up'; others wanted
ultimately to develop into family centres. A new headteacher
expressed her hope of making the school into a 'centre of learning for
all ages and a support network for parenting'.

Headteachers who welcome parents in after predecessors have
kept them out, find that the informal meetings are essential in
changing attitudes about the school and teachers. Some are available
at the beginning and end of the day, making themselves clearly
visible in the hall or playground and approaching parents rather than
always waiting for them to make the first move. Most infant school
teachers who want to, find it relatively easy to see parents as they are
collecting children at the end of the day. This informal approach,
although vitally important, does not reach all parents, however.
Many find that conversations tend to be about lost coats or falling
over in the playground, although immediate anxieties can often be
sorted out effectively.

There are always those who do not choose or do not get the
opportunity to come to school because of work or other commitments. This is always one of the chief anxieties when teachers believe
that they should see all parents in school. They sometimes blame the
parents, believing that they 'do not make the effort', despite the fact
that the school is always welcoming. Very young parents come in
for criticism when 'they shed their responsibility and want their
children cared for as much as possible by someone else'.

Teachers can also have mixed feelings about working mothers and
some complain about the amount of time children are away from
their families with childminders or at playschemes. Not only that;
those who are parents themselves need to get back home to their
own children. Since the majority of teachers in primary schools are
female, many have the same problems as the mothers of the children
they are teaching about childcare.

Teachers' individual perceptions and the way parents react to the
institution will obviously influence how they relate to each other.
For some schools, there is the 'them and us' syndrome which has to
be broken down after many years of inbuilt mistrust or bad experiences in schools. The language barrier and ways of communicating
also often inhibit teachers from going out of their way to involve
these parents. Some schools are in areas where there is a tremendous
turnover of families; in others, unemployment or bad living
conditions bring depression.

The idea of the school as a predominantly white institution is hard to get away from when the teaching profession itself is mainly white. There is still only a small percentage of black teachers. They can find themselves marginalized when they work on particular projects or are paid with special funds. They can also be under tremendous pressure when, as the only black worker, they are expected to deal with 'multicultural' issues.

The position of black staff in school has obvious implications not only for children but also for parents if they are only seen in subsidiary positions as meals supervisors, primary helpers or cleaners. The appointment of black officers and teachers with re-sponsibility will go some way to changing attitudes. But there is an inherent conflict in schools which teachers have to face. It is not enough for them to declare themselves anti-racist if the power relations do not change. If teachers are concerned because black parents are not getting involved in school activities then they need to stop and ask why. It is no wonder that parents who find their children failing in society or constantly underachieving have little faith in schools alone. Education is supposed to be the key to success, yet many have found that it has done little for them.

Where teachers understand the parents' concerns without being patronizing and also recognize their influence in their children's life then the school as an organization develops. It becomes a place where there are possibilities and choices not prescriptions. It is accepted that some parents are busy and not able to come into the school but this makes them none the less valid. If the school becomes a community resource where parents come for other things as well as their children, it is because this is wanted in the area not because these kinds of parents 'need' this. As the school adapts, relationships and routines will change. This may be hard at first and those involved may well need support and advice.

Schools which decide to be a resource for parents' activities as well as for children often have to re-examine their organization. Some teachers find it hard to give up control. Headteachers with overall responsibility for what happens in school can find it difficult to allow groups to take place without them. Adults do not conform easily. What parents want and what teachers believe may be 'good' for them may not be the same. And when running groups, there can be an underlying tension between what teachers see as the aim and how parents see it. There can be a problem of moving groups on, acknowledging that certain activities attract or need to be set up for particular people.

Primary school teachers are used to catering for everybody. That can be an asset for schools. Unlike social services, there is no stigma attached to using them. Thus when people ask for specialized groups many teachers are naturally reluctant and need to clearly understand their purpose. There was tension, for instance, in a school where the community teacher was running a group for women who had relatives in prison or had had bad experiences with the police. The headteacher was worried by the exclusiveness of a group that would neither accept newcomers nor liked the community policeman who visited the school. The community teacher was clear that this kind of group was needed in the particular circumstances. In a school where black parents had asked to set up a group specifically for them and in another where single parents had their own meeting time, head-teachers had to accept considerable criticism by others who felt excluded.

The school in the community

Many teachers believe that it is important for children to understand and feel that they belong in a wider society. And schools are constantly urged to get to know their immediate neighbourhood and maintain good relations with other agencies outside. Yet while acknowledging that it is a 'good thing' to involve the local com-munity, they have not always thought out the implications. De-fining who or what is the community is complicated. Is it the nurse, the policeman, the milkman who come into school, the fire brigade and ambulance workers who come and tell the children about their work? Or is it the families? Where do these begin and end? Can the cousins and aunts and friends come into the school and perhaps make use of the adult groups that have been set up? What about the pressure groups and local politicians giving their views about the local services including the school?

The community, as the extensive literature shows, is extremely difficult to define. If, as Milward (1983) has suggested, people see community education as tending towards 'notions of communal good life' and a consensus view, then they quickly become disillu-sioned or disaffected. If they see it as a natural way for people to look after each other then they may need to question whether community self-help can take place where there are massive economic, structural and cultural constraints (Finch 1983). Within the community that surrounds the school, there will be differences and conflicts.

Certainly no one would deny that it is important to create a warm and caring environment when working with small children. But the school is not a desert island. It is inextricably linked with a wider community from which its children come. Within this there are different cultures, traditions and values. As outreach workers and community teachers quickly learn, these differences, when acknowledged, make a positive contribution to the school, but they can also bring disagreement and conflict which have to be worked through.

Working more closely with the community is not just about doing things for people, offering services for which they will be extremely grateful. That is the easy part. It is also about being open and responsive to outside influences and other views, and it will mean change. Because some schools cannot or do not open up as a community resource, it does not necessarily follow that they ignore those outside it. Having adult classes or parents groups can be a way towards closer parental involvement, but if they are just 'attached' to the school they may make very little difference to the way teachers perceive others in their community.

On a purely practical level, it may not be possible for staff to spend a great deal of time outside the school. Teachers with full-time teaching commitments can rarely attend daytime meetings or visit other facilities in the area. Nor can they spend time running groups for adults in school. But what they can do is recognize that there is a world outside which will impinge not only on the children but on them as well. Moving from being the givers, the traditional role for teachers, to receivers is not easy if teachers do not know or accept that the community outside also has knowledge and experience to offer.

However much a school becomes less institutional, it is still an organization with a structure and functions. With the much tighter conditions of service for teachers and emphasis on a national curriculum, the kinds of informal link which many teachers have felt important can easily disappear. Thus it is important to see parental involvement both as what actually takes place within the school and what is happening without. Teachers may not like this, especially if it does not accord with how they believe the world ought to be. Yet since children spend as little as 20 per cent of their waking life in school, by denying there is a dynamic, influential community outside, they are ignoring a large part of the child's experience. Where all teachers, not just those working directly with parents, need training and support, is in confronting in a positive way the idea that although views and values in the community may be different, they cannot be ignored and may be perfectly valid. This is not easy when you have been trained to make schools places where everyone is encouraged to fit in and be happy. Allowing or indeed acknowledging conflict is not traditional in primary schools. Although most teachers are aware that it is there, they generally see it as something negative and, as Watt (1988) writes, 'are ill-equipped to handle it and would need considerable persuasion to believe that, if handled well, it could be a constructive and educational element in any institution with pretensions to community status'.

CHAPTER 6

Whose school is it, anyway?

'At the end of the day it's the head and deputy who run the school.'

(Parent governor)

In some ways, there now seem to be far more rules and regulations for schools to abide by than there used to. They have to produce brochures for parents; governors are required to hold meetings and discuss their annual report; teachers have to give information about pupils' attainment levels. At the same time, boundaries have shifted, roles have changed. It is not always clear who is accountable – governors, teachers, the local authority or the Department of Education and Science (DES). For the lay person the system is complicated. Misunderstandings continue. When new policies are put into practice, the norms and expectations of both parents and teachers may be challenged.

Translating written policies and educational theories into practice is an intricate process. As those who have to implement them know, they are not tablets of stone handed down but a set of ideas. New policies generally mean change and those in the thick of things may have had nothing to do with them. There may be a conflict of values; the practicalities have to be worked out; there can be strong resistance and disagreement about when and how policies should be implemented. People need explanations, time to absorb new facts, a commitment to implementing the new regime. It is easier to bring in new ideas collaboratively when they have been worked out within the school. What is more difficult is when they come directly from the Secretary of State or local authority. There will be minor issues as well as others with long-term consequences, affecting morale and practice, and schools can get caught in the crossfire when the government and local authority are at odds. They can also find that what they agree on as good policy is quite different from what is agreed in the school down the road.

Expressing opinions

Accepting that parents have the right to know and express their opinions after years of having been kept out is one thing. Putting this into practice is difficult, particularly when teachers worry about parents' increasing power. As Wragg (1989) suggests, however, giving parents rights is not synonymous with power:

> the right to be given a prospectus is not the power to say what should be in it, and the right of parents as a group to provide two to five parent governors is not the same as power to all parents to determine the conduct and curriculum of a school.

People need information and knowledge, the means to express their views and use their experience if they are going to exercise any power at all. Teachers sometimes believe that it is better for parents not to know when things go wrong or are problematic, although the chances are that they will get to know anyway. There is usually a strong 'grapevine' in every school which can cause a backlash if the information gets misinterpreted. Not telling parents what is happening can actually work against teachers for if parents do not know the pressures that are being put upon a school then there is nothing they can do. They are more likely to be sympathetic if they understand the context in which teachers must work. Governors, for instance, soon recognize the constraints once they are involved in budgeting.

Teachers who understand that parents' interest is primarily in their own children find that this interest progresses to a concern for the school. With information, parents can be, and usually are, powerful allies and friends. How this happens may well depend on how they are perceived by the school. For instance, some teachers are worried by over-anxious and pushy middle-class parents moving into gentrified inner-city areas and avoid them. Others see them as a new force in the neighbourhood who will take political action and get things done. Parents' appeals to politicians are far more effective than teachers'. A councillor or MP receiving a sackful of letters from protesting parents begins to think about the next election. As one 'potential ally' (Davis 1989) wrote: 'under LMS [Local Management in Schools] parents are going to be asked to fund-raise for necessities not luxuries, and it is unreasonable to expect such voluntary effort without reciprocal responsiveness to parents' concerns'.

Putting policy into practice

When schools begin to be more open then their troubles seem to begin. Macbeth (1988) describes this stage as one of 'professional uncertainty'. And, indeed, it is a time when teachers may feel uneasy about the way the information they are giving is being used, or disappointed at the parents' reaction. At this stage, those who have been clammering to get in come to the fore – suddenly there is a clique who dominate the PTA or are always in the classroom. Others do not like this. People who have never spoken out before begin to express their views. Old issues which had appeared to have died down, such as school uniform, are on the agenda again. Parents are asking questions, criticizing. They do not come for the 'right' reasons. Staff in one school, for instance, were delighted at the response to their request for help when children went swimming. They were less pleased when they discovered that parents were not offering for altruistic reasons but because they had been discussing how dangerous the swimming pool was and wanted to be sure of the facts. Teachers get hurt when parents are invited to come on an outing and then are only interested in their own children or do not stick to the rules. They are surprised when they refuse to come and tell a story in their mother-tongue, forgetting what an ordeal this may be for someone who is not used to working with groups of children. The 'goodwill' is severely strained when teachers find that the open-door policy is being taken literally by some parents who hang around smoking in the hall. And, as Edwards and Redfern (1988) found, they are initially disconcerted to find that parents do not behave as the children are expected to – they talk when the teacher is talking!

The temptation is to go back to the old ways when everyone knew what was expected, to avoid talking about differences or contentious issues and formulate neat regulations. Some parents – and teachers, too – still hold the image of the headteacher as the authority figure whose word goes. Using this power can indeed avoid trouble but does not allow change or real communication. It is all too easy to take the stance of one headteacher who was prepared to have a PTA in 'his new school' because there 'was not a lot of disagreement' but who had not encouraged one in his other school where groups had been more diverse.

Even small changes in policy can soon develop into full-blown debates if not acknowledged or thought out from the beginning. A typical exchange which I came across at the meat counter of a supermarket illustrates this. A group of mothers were discussing why the headteacher had changed the Christmas parties so that each class had them on different days instead of on the same day. 'It means I have to go three times for my children – I can't take the time off', said one. 'Why doesn't she ask us – it's always done for the convenience of the teachers', said another. The five of them decided to talk to other parents who were 'sure to agree' and 'tackle' the headteacher about this. I could imagine the scene next day as the head defended her actions against this deputation of by now irate mothers.

Opening the school up to the community so that there is easy access and understanding is an ideal, something to work towards. But teachers soon discover that the school does not operate in isolation; it is an integral part of a larger society which is also making demands. The policies introduced by the local education authority or the DES are often vague when it comes to the practice. Words such as democratization, choice and consultation can ring hollow in reality. When authorities just go through the motions of consultation, there is resentment on all sides. If conflict is not acknowledged and left to blow over, then it is likely to blow up later – probably in school. Tolerance and change do not happen overnight.

Principles at stake

There may be pressure groups outside who do not make their demands in conventional ways. Written off as troublemakers or not taken seriously by outside authorities, they become 'totally disillusioned with the education service' and make their demands direct to schools. The complaints become personalized. The teachers are the ones who are called to account. Yet what should they be accountable for? Shoring up schools that are cracking under staff shortages? Becoming more cost-effective and giving value for money with the need to give children a 'balanced and broadly based' curriculum? They may have a clear commitment to involving parents but also have to carry this out in a context where individual parents have very different values and beliefs and where local authorities or governing bodies have not thought through what it really entails.

Before being able to consult in groups, as those involved find out, much groundwork, negotiating and sharing information must be done to work out people's different expectations and perceptions so that understanding, if not always total agreement, can be reached. Those who really begin to do this cannot be vague or have romantic notions of harmony and peace. But they can work for greater understanding and exchange of ideas. Community values may be completely at odds with the school's; it may be difficult, or even impossible, for teachers to come to terms with the values that some of the parents hold. In some instances, they may find themselves having to challenge these or they may have radically to rethink assumptions which they have held for years.

A headteacher, recognizing this dilemma, emphasized the need to take the differences seriously when she said: 'Education doesn't stop with children; its lifelong and could lead to internal family conflicts. Trying to educate children and respect the wishes of parents has to lead to a dialogue so that the two can be done in tandem.' But being in 'tandem' can be extremely difficult where there are social, cultural and educational differences. There will be inevitable tensions and clashes which have to be recognized and faced up to. And being sure about group as opposed to individual rights is important where policies are not clear-cut.

There are legal requirements which people recognize as being part of the school rules. Attendance at school, for instance, is compulsory. It is the parents' responsibility to make sure that the child is there. Schools have a right and duty to complain when they do not carry this out. How they deal with this will vary, but they know they have the law on their side if they want to take action. There are other issues which are less definable. Certainly teachers cannot use corporal punishment and parents found to be physically abusing their children can be taken to court, but within any community there will be very different beliefs about discipline and how children should behave. A school will have guidelines about when to suspend children, but in the less extreme cases who is responsible for a child's behaviour in school is not always clear. Parents blame the school, teachers the home; the child is caught in between.

Where teachers see themselves working jointly with parents then they can begin to develop strategies. The following small but common incident shows that getting rid of the blame and treating each other as responsible adults immediately benefits the child. A mother whose child was not progressing was called in to school only to learn that it was because of her behaviour. She was naturally upset and at first took it as a personal insult. The teacher felt it was part of her job to demand high standards, and to help the child progress she said she needed support. The mother brought in her husband; the teacher, it seemed, was asking for trouble. But since she understood that there might be some initial anger, she did not take this as criticism. After much discussion, the parents talked about how difficult they found the child but how much they wanted her to achieve. It took time and several meetings, but they eventually began to talk about how they could work together. The teacher began to support them in getting the child to go to bed early; they became more interested in what she was doing at school. The child soon realized that the teacher and parent were working together and stopped playing one off against the other.

The more complicated policies to implement are those which are at the heart of a school's ethos. These may be based on educational principles or on political, moral or social grounds. They directly affect groups rather than individuals. Schools advocating equal opportunities, for example, may find themselves at odds with parents and other members of the community who have not considered the implications, do not see it as relevant to their children's schooling, or find the change threatening to the old order. But these issues need to be brought into the open or the ethos of the school can be severely undermined.

An anti-racist policy meant little in one school where a large majority of white parents, not explicitly boycotting a PTA meeting, nevertheless did not turn up because their candidate for parent governor had not been elected. In another, black parents came to the 'meet the teacher' part of a meeting organized by the PTA, but left when the social events and fund-raising events were discussed because they did not feel they were included. Knowing that there is likely to be a diversity of views and that confronting these issues will take time and demand big changes in attitudes means that teachers are tempted to ignore or cover up the conflict. But the uncomfortable feelings and unacknowledged differences do not disappear.

Headteachers can find themselves being criticized for 'doing everything for black groups' although, in reality, in most schools it is the white parents who dominate the parents' groups and governing bodies. Some schools who have printed an anti-racist policy in the school booklet and openly talked about this have found themselves in an invidious position. Prospective parents, having been shown the statement, have gone to another school which does not take as overt a stance on this. Although it is the authority's policy, parents have 'choice'. There is a clash between individual and group rights and they can undermine all that the school stands for.

Advocating equal opportunities in society which only pays lip-service to it in many places is a struggle for schools. They need parents to help and only by openly acknowledging a diversity of views can they begin to challenge and change opinions as people inside and outside the school begin to understand the implications of these policies. Children may be in a school where the walls have positive images and be introduced to multiethnic views, but if they go home to an environment that denigrates all this then little will be achieved in the long run. Parents may feel threatened, angry or see the emphasis on these issues as getting in the way of 'real' education. Others may complain that the policies are tokenistic.

Stone (1981) argues that black parents are much more concerned about their children getting a basic and formal curriculum than about 'multicultural' activities. This was expressed to me by a parent who said: 'I don't want all this wishy-washy liberal stuff. I want my child to learn the three *R*s.' But, as Tomlinson (1984) points out, the debate is not an 'either/or' one. The curriculum is inextricably bound up with how children see themselves. It expresses 'the basic power relationships of society as a whole' (Stone 1981). At present, the learning of the traditional curriculum, one which middle-class parents take for granted or have the choice to reject, is the way forward to careers which carry status and power.

Whose curriculum?

It is the mismatch between teachers' and parents' perceptions and values that has often got in the way when talking about curriculum. And despite being at the centre of their professionalism it is the area where teachers feel least confident talking to parents. Since the curriculum used to be mainly their responsibility they could easily focus on the apparently implicit criticism of their teaching methods when parents began to ask questions. The introduction of a national curriculum made enormous demands on them as they sought to make sense of it and of how their teaching styles fitted in. Many were concerned that it was a move backwards, going against educational principles which they believed in. The implementation of assessment procedures and schemes of work took up hours of time. For teachers who had been living and breathing it during the years before, discussing the implications of a national curriculum with parents was the least of their worries.

During its introduction in September 1989, a survey was undertaken to find out how aware parents were of educational changes in school. A total of 1887 interviews were carried out in two hundred local government wards. Only just over half of those interviewed had heard about it although, significantly, nine out of ten believed it was a good idea. The DES (1989a) booklet, *Our Changing Schools*, which was 'widely available' had only been seen by one in four parents. However, when asked, 94 per cent approved of attainment targets. Eighty-two per cent believed that assessments were also a good idea. Almost 100 per cent said they would welcome seeing the results of their children's assessment (Lodge 1989b).

The politicians' emphasis on poor standards has increased the worries of many parents whose children have been 'failing'. Much of the blame has fallen on the teachers. Thus from an outsiders' point of view, a national curriculum with laid-down attainment levels and assessment seems a way forward and a much simpler way of making teachers more accountable. Ironically, few teachers would disagree with parents that the basic subjects are important; it is over how these are taught that there is most misunderstanding. Despite the curriculum content being taken away from teachers, they have to translate it and put it into practice. According to statute, the main responsibility for raising standards still remains with them, the 1988 Act stating that 'legislation alone will not raise standards. The imaginative application of professional skill at all levels of the education service within a statutory framework which sets clear objectives will raise standards.'

Teachers' defensiveness about their professionalism has worked against them in the past, isolating them from parents and creating suspicion which politicians have been able to exploit with calls for accountability which are not altogether realistic. Yet as teachers know, education is not handed out like a dose of salts; it involves factors other than 'lessons'. They do not want to find themselves in a position where it is impossible to come up with the goods. As Sallis (1988) stresses: 'failures to understand make parents easy game for doorstep salesmen, peddling "you-add-the-egg" basic education mix'.

Parents' anxiety about their children's progress often stems from a lack of knowledge. Children are not generally communicative about what they have done at school and work taken home without explanation can mean little. The Thomas Report (ILEA 1985) on primary schools highlighted the need for information. Parents were worried by the lack of formal instruction, particularly in spelling and maths. Where they have been brought up on rote learning they will need convincing that other ways will also work. Although calculators and computers are now an accepted part of working life, it may seem like an easy option for young children unless people understand that they must already have some important mathematical concepts to be able to use them.

Despite a mandatory curriculum, it is just as vital that teachers discuss with parents what education, in its broadest sense, means, and involve them in it if their children are going to succeed in a system where there are so many factors which give children life chances and opportunities. If they do not share their practice with parents then it becomes an exclusive expertise. What happens then is that a child's 'failure' is put down to the teacher's inadequacy; parents are less likely to be involved in their children's schooling, seeing it as outside their responsibility. Either way the teacher is isolated in this kind of ownership. As Munn (1988) suggests, 'if a parent feels unable to talk to a teacher about the school's progressive spelling policy, then politicians' public worries about standards and the curriculum are more likely to find a sympathetic ear'. Thus teachers can find themselves caught in the middle, unable to satisfy anyone, becoming the scapegoat for everyone's discontent – the public, politicians, parents and children.

Together in the 'system'

The literature and teachers' accounts which focus on partnership as the ultimate aim sometimes leave out the differences and difficulties which have to be faced before this can be achieved. There is much 'in the system' which works against partnership and it is naive to think that by getting together with parents all this will change. Being more approachable and open also brings the need to be more self-critical, whether as parent or teacher. There will always be parents who are never satisfied, do not agree, or treat their children badly; there will be teachers like this, too. Teachers have to respond to pressures and beliefs from outside and introduce policies which may not always be popular with everyone. Decisions taken for the group may affect generations of children. Parents may find this difficult when their own child does not seem to get the best from this.

Some schools are clearly much less afraid of confronting conflictual issues and, indeed, build in a support system so that people can discuss and get used to new ideas and innovations. As one headteacher expressed it, being more consultative means 'you have to take the rough with the smooth'. But in doing this it is possible to get through the rough and move on in a dynamic, positive way rather than stagnate in negativity and ill will. Teachers and parents need each other in an increasingly complex educational 'system' where the main reason for getting together – the children – is sometimes lost as parents are asked to take on more managerial duties and teachers are being called to account for everything they do.

Both teachers and parents need support to carry out their responsibilities towards the children. Who better to help than the other main adults in their lives. Otherwise they turn to a system of legislation and theory sometimes far removed from the child's immediate needs. As Gibbons (1988) writes:

> It is curious that two Secretaries of State should be confident that unaided parents will be the salvation of the education service in this country. No-one would argue that parents should not have at least an equal voice with other groups, but the resources needed to make parent participation work are all missing. If it's so easy that we can all do it off the top of our heads, why have all those highly qualified educationalists made such a mess of it over the last few years?

Neither teachers nor parents should be expected to carry all the responsibility for what happens in the educational service. And putting the blame on each other is destructive and non-productive. Their strength together is considerable. They know what is actually happening; it is not theory, it is practice. By getting together they can begin to have a greater voice in what their children need today.

CHAPTER 7

In loco parentis

'A radical teacher is child-centred plus conscious of parents being working-class, unemployed, etc. – yet positive about the child's chances and abilities.'
(Community teacher)

Teachers walk into their classrooms each morning to be surrounded by a group of children for whom they are both *in loco parentis* and responsible for at least part of their education. Their role is a complicated one, 'fixed into the good of the child', and at the same time answering to the demands of society's concept of a 'proper' education – a concept which changes as theories are tried and tested and fashions come and go. If children needed 'nothing but Facts' and the teacher's job was to 'plant nothing else, and root out everything else', like Gradgrind's maxim in Dickens' *Hard Times*, then with the advent of computers, teachers would have a clear task to follow. But at the same time as delivering a curriculum of maths, language and science, the teacher has to take into account the isolated child, the bully and bullied, the one who is intellectually streets ahead and the one who lags behind.

It was Froebel in the nineteenth century who, reacting against the harshness of schooling for young children, stressed the importance of the humane – or, more specifically, maternal – qualities needed in teaching. He was among the first educationalists to emphasize the importance of the school and home coming together, and the need for the child to be nurtured as a 'Human Being'. His stress on a child-centred environment is at the base of early education theory (Froebel 1887). His belief in developing the whole child so that the physical, spiritual and emotional needs are given as much importance as the intellectual ones was radical at the time, though now almost taken for granted. The national curriculum, for example, 'promotes the spiritual, moral, cultural, mental and physical development of pupils at the school and of society' (Education Reform Act 1988).

Many of the pioneering educational ideas of the past, such as those of Froebel, Piaget and Montessori, have become part of educational lore. Most teachers will encounter these names and their respective theories during their training. Although these ideas certainly still hold good, there is also an inherent danger in the way they are interpreted. It must be remembered that they were put forward up to a hundred years ago when social conditions were very different. Froebel was writing when child-centred education was rare. His call for the teacher to become more like the mother who 'cautiously follows in all directions the slowly developing all-sided life of the child' was a reaction against the stifling of children's imagination and creativity in school.

The 'mother figure'

Few people would now dispute the importance of a 'mother' figure in a child's life. And in the twentieth-century primary classroom, there is the need for the teacher to take the double role of instructor and carer; indeed, there is concern that the national curriculum puts too much emphasis on the first to the detriment of the child's personal development. Nevertheless, it has to be remembered, as Steedman (1988) points out, that Froebel's concept of the 'mother made conscious' was tinged with the romantic ideas of Victorian childhood. He derived his concept from the middle-class mother in her nursery at home and the woman with 'natural' instincts of mothering. As Steedman argues, this 'romantic child-centredness' can affect, even unconsciously, both the way teachers see the children and the way they judge their parents.

This concept of the 'good middle-class mother' is still a powerful one in educational thinking. She is seen to have the right answers about how children should be brought up; she becomes the 'good' teacher. But underlying this is also the idea that since looking after children is a 'natural' instinct, then it is mainly a woman's job and it takes on the low status which goes with this. This double-edged concept of mothering leads to much of the current conflict between the teacher's and parent's responsibility. It allows persistent stereotypes and gets in the way of parents and teachers moving forward together.

Teachers inevitably find themselves caught up in these assumptions. On the one hand, looking after children is a natural ability most suited to women and therefore lacks status in the eyes of others. On the other hand, as 'mothers made conscious' they are called upon to provide the ideal conditions for children. When they find themselves in this impossible position, they naturally defend their professionalism. In turn, parents find themselves being deskilled by the 'professionals' and at the same time being judged on the mythical notion of the 'good' home. Parents feel let down because teachers are not able to change the structures to give their children a better deal; teachers blame the parents because they are not providing the kind of home a child needs to benefit from school.

Throughout this book the word 'parent' has been used purposely as a non-gender term. But it is, in fact, mainly women who get involved with primary schools. Women are usually the main carers; the majority of teachers are women and the proportion is increasing. There is very little mention of fathers in the literature on parental involvement. And child psychology mainly focuses on mothers. Although the attention is beginning to turn to fathers, in the past they have usually been defined by their working role rather than their fatherhood. Morgan (1981) notes that

> we know more about wives and mothers than about husbands and fathers; if the former are obscured from our vision by being too far in the background, the latter are obscured from our vision by being . . . too much in the foreground.

Significantly, even within work with children, which has low status anyway, there is an assumed hierarchy. It starts with being 'just a mother'. Those working with very young children come next. The first five years are the vital learning years in a child's life, yet nursery workers are among the lowest paid. Childminders, although providing the majority of childcare, have little money invested in their training and the job is often seen as one which almost any woman can do. Those who do not do it well are frequently blamed rather than helped. Primary teachers also rate low on the scale. There are far fewer opportunities for posts of responsibility than in secondary schools; primary schools are often viewed by the general public as places where children can coast along until the really serious business of education begins. The job fits in well with bringing up a family so can also be seen as a source of 'extra' income, a secondary job.

This idea of an implicit hierarchy in working with children has been around for a long time so can lead to assumptions which subconsciously influence people in the way they see their responsibilities. Overlaying the low status is also the ideal, the 'good' mother who is called on to be with her children full-time without seeking any reward other than their well-being. Parents are presented with this immediately a baby is born. The image is underscored by the media, the comparison with others who seem to manage better and the plethora of literature and experts, including friends and relatives, who are ever ready with advice. It is an 'ideal' which is impossible to live up to.

The focus on the mother figure reinforces many of the stereotypes which permeate society and which in turn influence how children see their place in it. Male teachers and fathers are cast as the authority or remote figures. Father comes up to the school only when there is trouble; it is assumed that the natural place for the male teacher is as a head or with older children. The single father struggles manfully; the single mother is expected to get on with it. Working with younger children is suspect or sissy. Theodoulou (1989), the only male worker in a nursery centre, asked fathers what they found difficult about coming in. A black father found himself cast in the role of 'macho provider'. When another suggested coming in, the head 'talked to him about the importance of not making the children too excited especially during outdoor play'. Theodoulou adds wryly: 'I wonder whether she would have had a similar conversation with a mother who had made the same request.'

The 'female' caring qualities of both men and women are debased. This relates directly to the children and how they perceive the adults around them. Boys are still encouraged to take on 'proper' jobs; working with children remains a 'nice' job for girls because it fits in well with the family. Teachers introduce anti-sexist strategies; they put up positive images on the walls and introduce stories which get away from the stereotypes. But schools professing equal opportunities cannot change the world alone – the dilemmas are common to parents and teachers, and they need to be acknowledged by them together. A 'mother made conscious', whether teacher or parent, becomes a mother aware of the child in a context outside the immediate home or classroom.

Distance and attachment

Many teachers are parents themselves, and experience the stresses, pride and strong emotional attachment to their children which the parents in their school will also be feeling. They will need to deal with their differing reactions as parents and as teachers. They may, as parents, find themselves being much more indulgent or, conversely, expecting much higher standards. Working with groups of children, there is not the same heightened attachment. Although they may be judged on how the children in their class perform, the responsibility of having 'naughty' children in it is not usually placed on them. The group needs have to be taken into account as well as the individual ones. As an outsider, it is easier to take a rational, detached view of what is happening to a child. Indeed, that can be a strength.

They will feel very differently about their own child who is not doing well at school. Their own naughty child is their responsibility. The child's behaviour reflects on them; he or she is a credit or 'shows up' the parents. The non-rational emotional attachment, wanting the best for your own child, is the parent's strength. But it is also a pressure. A parent cannot shed the responsibility at the end of the day. Women, especially, have to take account of their children even when they are working. Teachers whose children are ill during term time, for instance, have to make choices about their dual role of mother and teacher; they suffer the guilt of not being the 'good' mother who is always there to look after her own children.

As parents, they will defend their children to the last. They will say they know their children better than anyone. This is important, as Newson and Newson (1976) stress, for a child 'needs to know that to someone it matters more than other children; that someone will go to unreasonable lengths, not just reasonable ones, for its sake'. Naturally, teachers as parents want the best – particularly when it comes to education. All this they experience in their parent role. Yet so often they seem to forget this when faced by other parents, only really interested in their own child instead of the general workings of the school; the teacher role takes over.

It is the lack of clarity in the roles which engenders many of the conflicts. As Newson and Newson (1976) suggest, the relationships between parent and child and between teacher and child are very different. But 'because the roles have certain ingredients in common, though in different proportions (nurturance, discipline, information-giving for example) they are sometimes confused by the participants to the misunderstanding of all concerned'. Because of the nature of the job, teachers must inevitably distance themselves. Although encouraged to treat each child as their own, this is not possible where they must also be concerned with the group needs. But this 'distancing' can be difficult when there is a child in the class who is bruised or ill-nourished. 'I would support the child against anyone, though what I see as good for the child may not be the same as what the parent sees', said one teacher. This is where the clash comes, where the parenting role becomes uppermost and the balance between 'instructor' and 'carer' is unclear.

Parents, too, have this dilemma. They are legally required to hand over their children to other adults unless educating them at home. Thus they, too, must distance themselves and accept that the child will be one of many in school and no longer the main focus of the adult. There is tension when the child comes back home saying 'the teacher says' or 'in my school we have to . . .'. Their response can easily be 'well you can forget that – I'm the one who tells you.' Or if a child is not learning what is relevant to them or what they would expect, they feel excluded or angry. If this confusion about the responsibility is also overlaid by notions of a 'good' home or 'ideal' mother then the gap between teachers and parents widens even further.

Parents' interests

Research has shown that there is a difference between middle-class and working-class achievement. Much of this led to the belief that this was because working-class families could not provide the right environment for children to develop. What part the school played in these results was not always taken into account, so its main role was to compensate for the deficiencies of the home. Since the judgements were made from the perspective of the school the parents' interest in education was judged by their interest in the school rather than in their children. That is, parents who attended school regularly were, and often still are, judged to be taking an active part in their children's education.

There is increasing evidence to show that with very few exceptions the majority of parents, whatever their background, are concerned about their children and when asked to help educationally are eager to do so. In a study of parents and teachers in reception classes, Farquhar *et al.* (1985) found that although parents saw schools as playing a major role in determining academic achievement, the majority also believed that they had a definite role in helping their children educationally at home. Newson and Newson (1977), in their study of seven-year-olds in Nottingham, found that 81 per cent of parents, regardless of sex or class, were helping or had helped their children to read. Weinberger *et al.* (1986), in their discussion of a home reading scheme, found not only that the participation was high but also that there was no connection between the frequency with which parents heard their children read and social class. Nor did it make any difference whether they were second language families or single parents or whether there had been changes in the family's adult members.

It is because parents' interest neither is always immediately evident nor manifests itself in ways that teachers find easy to handle that some still believe that there are many working-class parents who are unlikely or unable to help their children. And where teachers place 'the greatest stress on the influence of the home, and family' (Farquhar *et al*. 1985) the children are then labelled 'disadvantaged'. This, as the study found, is at odds with parents, 'particularly black parents', who 'tended to attribute children's educational success, or lack of it, in part to the school'. This mismatch between minority parents' 'expectations with what the schools actually offer' (Tomlinson 1984) led to a widening of the gap. Not prepared to accept the argument that they were culturally and socially disadvantaged, they developed supplementary schools as a way to enhance their children's chances. Many teachers felt threatened by the exclusiveness of them and were critical of the extra pressure put upon children. Yet it was precisely because of their interest in giving their children the best possible chances that these were developed.

Even in nurseries where relationships between parents and teachers are often at their most informal, teachers are not always clear about the nature of their educational relationship. Tizard *et al*. (1981) found that many parents could not understand the emphasis on play in the nursery and that teachers equally found it difficult to put their views across. Parents were wanting specific advice on how to help their children at home, but most teachers were not willing to suggest ways or give out materials, arguing that giving activities to parents to carry out might 'overburden them or create anxiety, or result in too much pressure on their children.' Smith (1980) also found that there was much confusion about the role of parents when they came into the nursery. Although staff actively invited them in, there was little discussion about the children's activities and again the research highlights 'the mismatch between parents' expectations and teachers' objectives'.

With the past emphasis on the home's deficit rather than child's potential, it is easy to understand why teachers either believe that only they can compensate or that the children's chances are set down immediately they come into school. But if there is even a subconscious belief that the 'education' that happens at school is the real thing and the other at home is somehow not, then there is a long way to go before teachers and parents will really be able to begin to work together. For what they both have in common is the interest in the child. This is the starting point, the reason for getting together; other developments may come from this to the benefit of parent and teacher but there need be no other reason. It is a position of equality. Each has a responsibility in caring for and educating the child; the difference lies in the nature of these responsibilities.

A child–centred approach

As parents have been given a more central role in the education system much of the rhetoric has been about power and account-ability. The notion of partnership has become less about equality and mutuality and more about getting value for money. There has been little opportunity for discussion between parents and teachers about how this can practically happen, or indeed what it constitutes. Yet managing schools for young children is not just an academic exercise, as anyone involved as teacher or governor soon discovers. Children are not a commodity. They have a variety of needs and differing experience and ability. Both teachers and parents are bringing up children in a wider context than just the home or the school. Neither can be expected to provide everything. They are both subject to restrictions and perceptions which affect what they do and how the children respond.

The way forward is for parents and teachers to look at these tensions together so they can see those which are the same and those which are different. In doing this they not only give each other support but also begin to use them in a positive way to change things for the individual child and the group. There is inevitable conflict in both roles where the concentration is always on the ideal rather than the realistic. The realistic is attainable; the ideal pushes forward. Each is important but not to the exclusion of the other.

There can be a clash between the distanced and emotional views of a child, but the distant 'fair-minded' view and the emotional 'biased' view are the two sides of teaching and mothering; it is the propor-tions that are different. The child has only a relatively short time in school and, getting only one chance, needs the best possible one. Thus the parent, given information and resources, naturally does everything to get this – maybe to the detriment of others. But as Sallis (1986) points out, 'children's chances should not depend so decisively as they already do on the capacity of their homes to choose, to push, to support and supplement' so that it becomes a competition. And the distanced 'fair-minded' view is needed here to give the view of the rest of the group. This does not mean concentrating on the disadvantage, but rather an emphasis on the difference. It is a matter not of influencing childrearing practice or denying parents the responsibility for their children but of seeing children in a wider context where there are significant inequalities.

Getting away from the myth of the ideal and concentrating on what is actually happening, can mean using the tensions of distance and attachment productively. Teachers asking for higher salaries and more resources are not just demanding greater status; they are also questioning whether their work is as valued as, say, selling computers. The call is for a greater recognition of the importance of all children. And adults need skills, qualities, knowledge and support to be able to give them the best possible chance. Some of the qualities and skills needed are common for both teachers and parents. Some are not. But once they are valued realistically, they cease to be sentimental ideas which are irrelevant to adults and children alike.

Froebel's idea of the 'mother made conscious' becomes classless and can apply to both men and women. It carries with it educational knowledge and care. As teacher, 'she' wants the best for the child. She needs support to do this as well as opportunities to develop skills and expertise. As parent 'made conscious', 'she' wants the same. This does not mean being told that there is only one approach, a textbook formula. But she needs access to information and opportunities to share her views on a child's development. Like the teacher, the parent needs status. Becoming 'conscious' takes away the isolation, the guilt; it is the way to improve what is being offered to the child; this can then can become a joint enterprise. It is a child-centred approach.

PART III

Talking together

It takes more time and effort and delicacy to learn the silence of a people than to learn its sounds.

(Ivan Illich, from 'The Eloquence of Silence')

Although I recognize that a whole-school approach to working with parents is important, I believe that the interaction between individual parents and teachers is also crucial. Most teachers admit that they have little difficulty in talking, but that when it comes to listening this takes skill and practice. Part III therefore looks at the communication that takes place between parents and teachers and offers some practical ways to improve it.

The chapters can be used separately as starting points for discussion with student teachers or for in-service training. Some exercises are included but it should be stressed that these are examples, not a comprehensive training programme. They may be used as a basis for role play or as preparation for the real thing. Either way, they are there to give participants experience of how inseparable listening and talking should be.

CHAPTER 8

Communicating with parents

Communication techniques are gaining in importance as schools become involved in public relations, selling, and attracting customers. Marketing skills for headteachers are now part of management courses. Brochures look more and more professional as teachers gain access to desk-top publishing. It is the image, the public face which is important here. Whether this ultimately improves the personal relations between teachers and parents is questionable.

However glossy and professional the school brochure, it is, in the end, the interaction between individual teachers and parents which is of paramount importance. The children are the primary reason for getting together and it is the common interest in these which makes the relationship so special. Where home–school relations are developing positively it is the nature of the communication, the confidence that teachers have to disclose information or take on conflicting views which is at the heart of this. Getting together is not about friendship, although this may develop; it is a vital working relationship.

People often claim that the good listener or communicator is born, not made. Certainly some find it easier to communicate than others, but there are nevertheless skills which can be practised and learned. How teachers give messages, convey ideas and how the parent receives them will have a tremendous effect on what happens to the child. Communication is not just about words, but is influenced by where it takes place, the non-verbal cues, the way words are used.

Teachers will be communicating with parents for all sorts of reasons: to give and receive information, to discuss what they are doing, to get a better understanding of a child, to give advice, to work together. At times, they will be called upon to help. Deciding what this help should be can be problematic, especially when it does not seem to relate directly to the child. 'I'm not a social worker', say teachers in despair who feel that parents are talking to them too frequently.

Teacher as 'counsellor'

Helping each other is a normal part of human experience. Whether we be friend, parent, shopkeeper, doctor or teacher, people are going to ask our advice at some time or other. There will always be an element of 'counselling' in teaching. The children themselves are going to need explanations about the world they live in, the way people behave. Adults, too, will be asking questions and sometimes seeking help. When discussing a child's development or talking about what is happening in the family and how this affects the child, the teacher will be 'helping'. This does not mean giving instant advice, having the perfect answers. But if taken seriously, it will mean understanding one's role and influence, examining one's own values and looking at how one expresses oneself effectively.

Egan (1986) sets out the different types of helper and clearly distinguishes between those whose main job it is to counsel, such as psychotherapists and social workers, and those who because of the nature of their job will be called upon at moments of crisis. As he suggests, many who help incidentally, such as hairdressers and bartenders, are often proud to be able to do so. It is perhaps because those in the 'caring' professions are not sure where the boundaries begin and end that they are sometimes worried about what they should offer. Some teachers with a particular interest attend counselling courses and find this useful when working. But I believe that listening skills are so much part and parcel of a teacher's job that they should not be seen as only for the specialist. And as Egan writes, 'since interpersonal helping is such a common experience, one wonders whether some kind of training shouldn't be as common as training in reading, writing and math.'

Professionals are often deemed the experts, partly because they have wished to be seen as this but also because others find it comforting to invest them with god-like knowledge. Yet this can be a hindrance. The issues which teachers and parents talk about do not always have simple answers. Discussing why a child is disrupting a class or having nightmares is very different from suggesting which book to take home to read. A child's development does not take place in a straightforward way; one has to look at factors inside and outside school.

It would be much easier to tell parents to 'keep on taking the pills' when they ask advice. But as more and more doctors are recognizing, physical and psychological symptoms are inextricably interlinked. Just handing out pills can create dependency or give short-term relief but the underlying problem may not have been tackled. The 'Balint' approach to general practice, described by Pendleton *et al.* (1984), is particularly relevant to teachers who find themselves wanting to come up with a simple diagnosis rather than taking a more holistic approach. It emphasizes the need for doctors to take into account their 'feelings, thoughts and prejudices' during consultations. It does not deny the importance of the diagnosis but stresses the importance of the relationship between the doctor and patient and how this affects the interaction. It shows that 'doctors are able to treat bodies and minds simultaneously' and that 'it is impossible to look at a relationship whilst taking into consideration just one of the persons' (Pendleton *et al.* 1984).

Giving advice is a two-way process as teachers and parents explore problems or ways of changing together. It requires teachers to listen respectfully, be genuine and, above all, empathize. A parent, angry about the kind of help she had received from different professionals, summed up the sensitivity that is needed when she said:

> they should start from the point of understanding the frustration you're feeling – it's not just the child, it's you being frustrated at the whole situation . . . You might not think what you are saying is harmful . . . you're treading on an emotional minefield (Silverman and Stacey 1989).

Looking at ourselves

For many teachers, actually talking is not the problem. They are used to doing this. Much more difficult is the listening, the letting go of control, the sharing of information, the admission that they do not, nor should always be expected to, have all the answers. Becoming less controlling is what many teachers find hard. One of the primary concerns for a classteacher is to 'keep order'; she is often judged on the way she organizes a class of children. 'Once a teacher always a teacher' is a common phrase and it is easy to fall into the trap of organizing everyone else as well as the children and thus taking away responsibility. One has only to listen to teachers' exasperation with social workers when they do not tell families what to do. Yet, as I have found when working with social workers, the more reflective approach of the latter combined with the active one of a teacher can be of great strength and bring new perspectives on a situation.

In looking at how we communicate we have first to look at our own behaviour and how that affects what we are saying. This is not always comfortable and it may mean changing attitudes. But acknowledging feelings of anger and anxiety allows one to be less defensive and to communicate more honestly. We often overlook the importance of emotional skills in working with people. As the emphasis in the education service is increasingly on results, so intellectual competence is seen as one of the most important skills. Thus the 'management of words and ideas, figures and objects earns acclaim – the skill of handling expression of feelings competently within human relationships has become irrelevant' (Dickson 1982).

In-service training has, in the past, often focused on doing rather than being. Quite naturally, teachers under pressure ask for quick answers, a formula or pack. But a good 'listener', 'counsellor' or 'teacher', whether with children or adults, will find the learning an ongoing and, at times, uncomfortable process. The developing teacher is permanently uneasy – that is, self-critical – seeking further knowledge, not pat answers, yet at the same time valuing her own experience as part of the learning process. In order to develop the 'emotional skills' as well as the intellectual ones, she will need support and a trusting environment.

Reflecting on one's own behaviour helps in understanding others. In his explanation of the theory of 'personal constructs', Kelly (1955) makes a comparison between how individuals understand what is happening to them and how scientists create hypotheses to work out experiments. Each person will construct a view of the world so as to make sense of it. This understanding will depend on past experiences and will in turn affect the present behaviour. Since each person's framework will be unique because the theories will have been constructed differently, reactions and behaviour will vary. But it is not static because, as Kelly suggests:

> The universe is real; it is happening all the time; it is integral; and it is open to piecemeal interpretation. Different men construe it in different ways. Since it owes no prior allegiance to any one man's construction system, it is always open to reconstruction.

Understanding one's own behaviour in this way makes it easier to recognize why others react as they do. This does not imply making judgements; rather it helps people to be more explicit about their own behaviour and how it affects others, and, as Davis (1985) suggests, 'because it equates all behaviour, whether that of a scientist, counsellor, parent or child, it is a very respectful model'. As we begin to acknowledge our own strengths and weaknesses then we can begin to respect and forgive ourselves. In doing this we can then move towards trust, respect, forgiveness and honesty towards others.

Barriers to communication

Previous chapters have already identified some of the constraints which inhibit parents and teachers. Some of these are more difficult to overcome than others, such as the structures imposed on schools as institutions. But it is possible in face-to-face contacts to become more aware of what barriers both parents and teachers put up. Even the best of communicators will experience these difficulties at times.

The following are some examples of what can go wrong and why. They are offered as a basis for discussion.

- Lack of trust. This can be historical; parents and teachers come with preconceived ideas about each other. Parents can feel on the defensive – sometimes because of their memories of school. Those who did not like it or had 'problems' will find it difficult if they feel their child is undergoing the same experience.
- Distance. This is not just a physical barrier but can develop because of superior or inferior attitudes. Distance can be created by the words; you feel you are being talked down to. Jargon, sometimes used inadvertently, excludes. Not giving the other person an opportunity to speak or give an opinion establishes positions which are difficult to move on from.
- Lack of clarity. This happens when people are defensive, anxious, preoccupied or an argument erupts. People are sometimes not clear about what it is they want to say until they get started.
- Distortion of the message. The message can get distorted when the sender is not clear yet expects the receiver to understand. Sometimes there are not sufficient explanations or examples. It may be that the person giving the information talks too fast or a strong emotion such as anger or anxiety overrides the message. Sometimes the receiver blocks out or does not want to accept what is being said.

- Making judgements. The listener begins to judge the speaker in terms of whether she agrees or disagrees, whether what he is saying is good or bad, relevant or irrelevant. It is not necessary to agree with everything. But if these judgements get in the way of hearing what is being said then the discussion may not move on, explore new ideas or resolve any conflicting views.
- Distractions. There are frequently many external distractions when adults are talking together in school. Children need attention; there is noise or pressure of time. It is also possible to be distracted by one's own preoccupations, the appearance of the person or similarities and differences of experience. Listening takes a great deal of concentration.
- Biases. It is virtually impossible to listen without bringing preconceived ideas and personal interpretations. It is therefore important to be aware how cultural differences can inhibit listening. Psychological or political beliefs will also be influences as well as parents preconceptions of what teachers are like. Some parents may 'submit' or co-operate because that is how they see their role with teachers. This can be just as inhibiting as those who feel naturally aggressive towards teachers.
- Over-identifying. What the person says arouses the listener's sympathy so much that it distorts what he or she hears. 'I know just how you feel' may sound reassuring, but can actually stop the person from expressing and thus beginning to understand the feeling.

Who is a good listener?

Active listening means giving attention and taking in information. It takes more effort than many people realize. Developing listening skills during in-service training can help teachers become more aware of what they do with parents and children and help improve concentration. Below are listed some skills which can be developed with practice.

- Giving attention. Listening means giving attention physically and mentally. The body will show how involved the listener is and physical attention will help the speaker psychologically and emotionally.
- Showing interest. Research has shown that over 70 per cent of communication happens non-verbally. Eye contact, facial expressions, head and body gestures will all reveal how much the listener is in touch with what is being said.

- Clarifying. Making sure you understand helps concentration. It also gives the speaker an opportunity to sort out ideas. Asking people to repeat something with such phrases as 'I'm not sure I've understood that' or 'Can you tell me again the bit about . . .' puts the onus on the listener. It avoids making people feel inadequate about the way they have expressed themselves. Clarifying helps to avoid misunderstanding from the beginning.
- Reflecting back. Good listeners reflect what a person has said and show that they have heard. Their reflections are genuine and specific not a clichéd 'I hear what you say'. Reflecting back the feeling a person seems to be expressing gives him or her a chance to deny or confirm this and also think about it.
- Drawing out without questions. The teacher question and answer trap is easy to fall into. Direct questions can be threatening because one may not want to answer them. They can also stop the conversation developing. Open statements and questions give the speaker choice and an opportunity to discuss other thoughts and ideas.
- Summarizing. This is particularly important for teachers when ending discussions with parents so that any misunderstandings can be cleared up. It can be done together. Summarizing during a discussion can also be helpful as it avoids constant interruption but also shows genuine interest in being clear about what has been said.

When teachers have not been used to practising listening, they can feel self-conscious and inhibited. It is important therefore that these skills are seen in the context of general personal development and not just as professional techniques or quasi-counselling which can be learnt in one easy session. They are one way of improving discussions between parents and teachers, to give confidence and more awareness. But, as Egan says, 'The goal of listening is understanding.' That is what anyone in partnership is ultimately looking for.

CHAPTER 9

Meetings with parents

If meetings are just left to chance then communication can go badly wrong or never really develop. Words can be misinterpreted because they are spoken at a busy or inconvenient time. Irritation sets in when teachers feel that the same parents want their attention every morning. Parents complain that they are not given time or find themselves talking over a hubbub of voices. Some teachers appear to have a natural ability to get on with parents; they are seen chatting and laughing, always ready with a joke or quip, the life and soul at the social evenings. Others have the 'please do not disturb' look and, busy with important looking activities, rush off when approached.

What's the purpose?

Setting aside time to look at the purpose of meetings between parents and teachers and what actually goes on is extremely revealing. Teachers who feel shy or intimidated by parents can be helped towards much better two-way communication as they plan more carefully what they want to discuss with parents; the extroverts may find that they are not necessarily better communicators of information. People begin to realize how they tend to avoid giving 'bad' news or situations where parents might be 'difficult'; they notice the excuses they make for not saying anything, such as destroying a previously 'good' relationship or parents' lack of understanding. But they also see how not saying anything often allows situations to deteriorate even further.

Below are some practical exercises and questions for discussion. These can be used individually or in groups. Where there are opportunities to role play, this can help teachers understand what it is like to be on the receiving end. It should be said, however, that role play needs skilled facilitators who understand the support that people may need when looking at their own feelings.

What are you wanting to communicate?

This may seem an obvious question, but it is surprising how often teachers have not really thought out what they want to say. If you are giving information about the child's development how specific is this? Why are you telling the parent? So that she can help? To alert her to possible difficulties that the child might have? To assure her or inform her?

How will you check that the parent has heard what you have said?

You may need to check that the parent has understood what is said by repeating it. This is not doubting a person's intelligence. But someone who is anxious or annoyed does not always find it easy to listen. We all block out what we do not want to hear. People need time to think, to digest facts. Even if it is straightforward information that you are giving, you need to be sure that there are no misunderstandings. Above all, you need to avoid jargon.

How will you introduce what you want to say?

The tone you set will be crucial to the rest of the meeting. There is a difference between beating around the bush and not getting to the point and starting: 'Now, this is what I have to say to you.' It is important to introduce the reason for the meeting and also give parents time.

Where should the meeting take place?

Where will you both feel most at ease? The classroom or head-teacher's room is not always the best place for discussions. There is often a need for a neutral place where you can speak as equal adults and discuss issues you may not agree on. Privacy is important, too.

How will you give the parent the opportunity to ask questions?

It is a natural feeling to want to avoid questions which will be difficult to answer. But if these discussions with parents are going to be more than lip-service then there needs to be opportunities to talk about differences and to follow up questions which you cannot answer at once. It is easy to find yourself in a defensive position or trying to justify an action. It is much better to acknowledge that you are finding it difficult to answer a question or are uneasy about talking. Then a real dialogue can begin.

How will you check that you have understood what parents have said?

Probably one of the greatest complaints from parents is that teachers do not listen or do not understand. So they see no point in talking to them. Summarizing what someone has said helps them to know you have heard. Ask questions to clarify. Avoid rushing in with your answer. Think about what has been said to you in previous discussions.

Talking about the curriculum

'Assessments will bring out strengths and weaknesses. Parents can discuss their children's progress with teachers and talk about what needs to be done next', said the National Curriculum Council guide for parents (1989). It sounds so simple, yet discussing the curriculum is not just talking about subjects. Teachers can be intimidated by parents who appear critical about everything that they are doing or not in the least interested. Parents can feel powerless or at a dis-advantage. Positions get taken up and the discussions become a kind of ritual, particularly if they only take place at open evenings, with both feeling ill at ease.

A young teacher, worried about what to talk about to parents, asked her head what to say. 'Ask them', he replied. Certainly this was sound advice since the trap for many teachers, especially if they are nervous or defensive, is to fall into a monologue allowing occasional comments. Atkin's and Bastiani's (1985) transcripts of parents and teachers talking show this only too well. Parents also complain about pat answers; as one parent put it, 'I think they tell you what they think you want to hear.' Using children's work or own words to illustrate what they have been doing can help to break down initial uncertainty and focus the discussion on them. Talking about what the children do at home, how the parent regards them, is also important if the teacher is not to be cast into the role of 'expert' working on a higher plain.

Partly because teachers themselves were inundated by new language to describe old practices, a new educational jargon has been built up which means very little to the uninitiated. Lessons are 'programmes of study'. How much a child knows is a 'level of attainment'. Initials such as LEA, DES, LMS, used as short cuts, can easily baffle and titles such as adviser and education officer mean little to most parents, who are not aware of what they do. The school psychologist can strike terror into the heart of a parent unless introduced with an explanation. Teachers need to check that these words, taken for granted in the staffroom, do not become a form of defence or exclusive. Having to ask what words mean can make the most assured parent feel ignorant and put down. It is important that parents know what 'core' and 'foundation' subjects actually mean in terms of the time spent on them and what teachers are expected to teach. These words are laden with meaning and how they are interpreted will affect the way teachers and parents go on to talk about their expectations.

In planning any discussion but, in particular, when it is around the curriculum, teachers need to be clear that parents not only get a chance to ask what they want but also receive information which is relevant to their child and useful for them in helping and encouraging. As one parent put it: 'I have a fair idea of what he's doing in school. The only thing I wouldn't know is whether he's good, behind or just average.'

Below are some questions for teachers to discuss either among themselves or with parents. For what is important in any dialogue with parents is not that teachers should account for everything that they do with the children but that they should give parents an opportunity to learn more about what their individual children are doing and how they can help.

- What is different about the curriculum today when parents were at school? People find it easier to talk from their own experience. They need to know why teaching methods have changed.
- What words are now in the educational vocabulary that were not there five or ten years ago? Consider such words and phrases as

'resources', 'national curriculum' and what these mean to you as well as to parents.

- How will a parent find out how a child is getting on if they do not hear from the teacher? They will ask the child, talk to other parents, look at the books, writing, pictures that a child brings home, compare other children, read books about what she or he 'ought' to be doing.
- How will the teacher's view of the child add to this information?

Giving 'bad' news

Parents of children with special needs, asked why they valued certain professionals, said that it was because they told the truth, treated them with respect and dignity and listened sensitively (Silverman and Stacey 1989). This did not take the pain or distress away but their feelings were acknowledged. What angered them was any perceived arrogance or being passed on so that they never got an answer. As one father put it: 'We saw almost everyone except the Queen Mother!'

Telling the truth is not always easy and thus we avoid it or get angry about being placed in an awkward situation. If teachers really want to work together with parents, they will have to discuss sensitive issues such as when a child is not developing, if there has been an accident, or difficulties in school.

Exercise

Think of a situation where you have to tell a parent something negative. Find one which is relevant to you. It might be that a child is not reading, has hit another child or is crying a lot in school. Or you may want to suggest referring the child to an educational psychologist.

Ask yourself the following questions and if possible practise the situation so that you can begin to experience your feelings as well as get feedback on how it felt receiving this news.

1. How will you be feeling? Nervous? Angry? Intimidated? Anxious? How does this affect what you have to say? How does this feeling get expressed? Through the words you use, your body language, your voice?
2. What practical arrangements will make meetings easier? How much time have you set aside for discussion? Have you

thought out where will be the best place to talk? How will you suggest going somewhere else other than the classroom? Have you thought about the arrangement of the furniture? For example, will you be sitting on children's chairs, will there be a table between you? What difference will it make if you are sitting or standing?

3. Can you give details of the child's observable behaviour rather than general opinions? Can you give specific examples? These are important starting points for giving joint help to the child and avoiding criticism.

4. How do you think the parent will be feeling? Why? How do these feelings affect you? Do you find yourself becoming defensive, protective or vague?

5. How will you give the parent the opportunity to give his or her opinion?

6. What is the way forward? There may not be an easy answer but you need to talk about what happens next. Will you need to meet again, get further information, come to an agreement about the role each of you will take on?

7. How will you end? Are you both clear about what has been said, what each is going to do? Can you end on a positive note? This may be an expression of relief or thanks, or a look at what the child has already achieved.

Dealing with conflict

Any conflict is likely to bring anxiety, anger or a loss of confidence. Accepting these feelings as natural rather than pretending that they do not exist goes some way towards dealing with the stress and beginning to face the problem. Understanding why we find conflict difficult can help us feel more confident and therefore more open when people come in to complain. Below are some questions to consider, with some examples.

1. Look at what brings the conflict. Is it differing perceptions of a child's behaviour; broken 'rules'; parent's treatment of the child which differs from the teachers; lack of information; misunderstanding; different values?

2. List the differences between parents and teachers and consider how this affects the way they perceive the child.

Parent	Teacher
Highly emotional	Needs some distance

Interest in own child	Sees individual child in groups
Knowledge about own child	Knowledge about children in general
Responsible 24 hours	Specified hours
Copes with everything	Specific responsibilities
Wants the best for own children	Wants the best for all children
Job other than with children	Chose to work with children

3. Look at what is frightening about conflict. For example, there may be anger, even violence, your relationship with the child could deteriorate, the consequences may be difficult to deal with or your authority could be badly undermined. Consider what frightens you most.

4. How do you avoid differences? Do you pretend they do not exist? Lay down rules which have to be obeyed? Try to be 'nice' all the time? Complain or take it out on others? Have someone else deal with the difficulty like the home–school liaison teacher or the headteacher?

5. What is the ideal solution? The child leaves, goes into another class, the parents do exactly what you say or someone else deals with the situation? Compare this with the realistic solution. Looking at this means that you do not avoid the situation and, more importantly, you can take some action to change it. This may only be short-term or merely an acceptance that there is a difficulty but it stops the 'if only . . .' thoughts which can waste so much time.

6. In accepting that there will sometimes be conflict, what help do you need when you are having to deal with difficult people or are under stress? Where can you get support?

Handling criticism

'If I open the school up then I open myself up to criticism', said one headteacher. Yet 'it seems a nonsense if teachers and parents don't know each others' expectations'. Giving and receiving criticism is not easy, nor is it part of the way teachers and parents have been brought up to talk with each other. But there is a need to make disagreements acceptable so that discussions about children become worthwhile, and there can be more sharing of ideas. Where there is no acknowledgement of differing ideas or opportunity to discuss them then what so often happens is that parents complain away from the school, or do not believe there is any point in talking to the teachers. Rather than seeing criticism as purely personal, it can also be a way forward towards understanding, to hearing a different point of view. Both views, after all, can be equally valid.

Handling criticism cannot be learnt with a few instructions as there are many deep feelings involved. And I would recommend teachers who want to handle difficult situations without growing aggressive or losing confidence to do some training in assertiveness (see Back and Back 1982; Dickson 1982). The suggestions below serve as a basis to begin to look at how you might handle a situation differently.

1. Listen carefully. One of the most important but difficult things to do is to actually listen when someone is being critical. Since our experience of criticism has generally been negative, we tend to defend ourselves with a counter-attack or immediately blame ourselves. Either way, we begin to cut off from what is being said.
2. Make sure you're clear about what is being said. Criticism is an opinion; it may not be fact. There will be many different opinions amongst parents as well as staff.
3. Think and breathe before responding – don't jump to conclusions. The criticism may come as a personal attack. It may be about something which is outside your control. For instance, parents are likely to get angry when the school keeps closing because of lack of staff.
4. Respond honestly to what is being said. There will be criticism which is true. If you believe it is, then, as difficult as it may be, acknowledge this. It does not mean that you have to demean yourself. But be straight about it; offer an explanation rather than excuses. Do not immediately shift the blame to someone else. It may be partly true. Again, listen carefully and give a short explanation.
5. Take the criticism seriously. If it is untrue, disagree but be brief and specific. Do not get into a long argument or numerous justifications.
6. Show you understand. It may be that there is no immediate solution. Allow an opportunity to talk about this. Find out why a parent is feeling dissatisfied, upset or frustrated.
7. Focus on the facts of the problem rather than getting caught up in the emotion. While it is important to acknowledge your own and

the other person's feelings, it is important that these do not get so much in the way that you cannot move towards a solution.

Exercise

1. Think of a situation you have met where you have been annoyed or upset by a parent or parent's attitude. Describe it to another person or small group. Why were you annoyed or upset? Try to analyse the reasons carefully. The following questions may help you and the group may think of questions too. Was it personal? You do not like the person or feel threatened or superior to them? Was it because they were critical of you or what you are doing with the children? Was it because they disrupted the routine? Was it on account of the child?
2. Imagine you are now the parent. Go through the situation and describe it from his or her point of view.
3. Why do you think the parent was annoyed or upset?
4. Why do you think the conflict arose?
5. Do you think you were justified in feeling angry or upset? Do you think the parent was?
6. How would you deal with the situation if it arose again? If possible, practise the situation as a role play.

Talking with parents – a summary

- Be honest and specific.
- Be flexible. Seek the parents' opinion so that you can work together on solutions and ideas.
- Observe carefully. Notice how you are feeling and how that is affecting the discussion. Recognize that parents may be feeling inhibited or tense and give time for them to take in what you are saying and offer their views.
- Listen. Concentrate and show you are listening by adopting an appropriate posture and by seeking clarification, reflecting and summarizing.
- Help the parents relax. They are on your territory. Give them a chance to contribute to the conversation.
- Allow silences for thought and reflection. Many of us have been brought up to believe that silences are awkward. Yet talking can be an interruption and disruptive. Silences allow people time to collect their thoughts and continue.
- Be positive about the child. Give examples, not generalities.

- Ask questions which lead the conversation on. Avoid putting answers in the parent's mouth. Allow questions which are difficult or challenging for you.
- Answer questions honestly. Avoid justifying or going on the defence. If it is difficult for you to say, express the feeling. If you do not know the answer then admit this. Do not make promises which you know you cannot fulfil or reassure with improbabilities.
- Remember, good relationships take time. Allow the relationship to grow. It is not friendship but a viable working partnership that you are seeking. This does not mean that you have to agree on everything but it means you need to respect and value each other's experience.

CHAPTER 10

Visiting parents at home

Several teachers, particularly those in nurseries and reception classes, have taken up the idea of visiting parents at home enthusiastically. Many have been encouraged by the results of home visiting schemes where teachers or volunteers have worked over a long period with parents. Most of these have focused on families with children under five or with special needs. They became increasingly popular in the 1970s when research such as Bronfenbrenner's (1974) showed the positive long-term effects of teachers and parents working closely together.

Some teachers are based in schools as educational visitors, working with parents and preschool children in the neighbourhood. They make regular visits to families, run groups and toy libraries, liaise with other services and act as a link between home and school. Others working with under-fives are part of adult and community education or voluntary schemes. Poulton (1983) describes how the first educational visitors appointed in the 1970s all acknowledged the importance of parents' educational role and the need for partnership. Yet their roles varied considerably, depending on the underlying philosophy of those administrating the schemes. Some mainly concentrated on preparing children and their parents for school; others were more involved in family 'problems', especially where there was stress or adverse circumstances.

What most educational visitors soon learn is that the specific educational element in their role is often blurred with a more general supportive one as well. They have to develop a flexibility which takes account of the varied needs of parents with young children. It is a humbling experience for many visitors who come from the classroom to realize that not only do they frequently not have the answers but they may not even have begun to ask the right questions. Grant (1989) gives a graphic account of her learning as she worked with parents in Glasgow and the painful awareness she sometimes had to go through as she began to be 'able to laugh at [her] ridiculous hope that a problem which exercised the minds of international educationalists would be solved by a little ten-week home-made course'.

The role of the full-time home visitor is very different from that of the teacher who goes to the home occasionally and this section focuses on classteachers or those with a few sessions set aside for home–school liaison responsibility. Nevertheless, many of the same questions have to be addressed. Home visiting, as many teachers discover, is not a panacea; it is not an easy way for home and school to move closer together. If teachers believe that it will be a helpful way of developing links with parents, they need first to examine why being in someone's home is best, then what it is they are offering and how this should be done.

Smith (1975) described the qualities needed for a home visitor as

> unbiased, non-judgmental, able to work under any sort of conditions, knowledgeable without being dictatorial, helpful without being patronising, able to listen, and sensitive to people's needs without appearing to probe into their private affairs.

Although he is referring to those working full-time, his definition highlights the importance of teachers' attitudes, too. What is crucial for anyone visiting is to understand that they have no 'right' to be there. Thus a suggestion to visit a parent at home should be made so that they feel they have the option to say 'no'. Few are likely to refuse but being given a choice means that they have some control over what is happening.

Most teachers, particularly those in reception or nursery classes, visit in order to introduce themselves or give information about the school. They find this a useful way of making an initial contact with parents and children will see a familiar face on their first day. Inexperienced teachers can find themselves in an uncomfortable position, particularly since schools are increasingly involved in public relations, if they are not reasonably informed about school policy nor have any knowledge of the child. They should at least know the name and age of the child or the visit can become like doorstep sales as teachers, laden down with carrier bags of 'samples', annual reports or worksheets, show off their wares. A good role model for a first visit is that of the neighbour greeting the newcomers, welcoming them in and giving them some useful information to help them become familiar with the area.

Advantages and disadvantages

There is no doubt that home visiting can bring much closer links between some parents and teachers. Parents are on their own ground. They are in a powerful position; they can decide whether to open the door and invite the teacher in and when to terminate the visit. They host the situation. Those who can never come into school because of work and other commitments appreciate the time given to them to discuss their children. Seeing parents at home when they are involved in educational projects such as reading schemes both gives opportunities for more extended discussion and visibly demonstrates the importance of the learning that takes place there.

Some parents find it easier to go into school after a visit and most children enjoy the fact that their teacher has been to see them. Misunderstandings can sometimes be cleared up in an informal setting. Teachers take the initiative, make the effort, rather than 'demanding' to see the parent at school. A child's continuous absence, for instance, can be dealt with before it turns into a formal complaint. Talking about the child is more private and personal. Parents intimidated by the school setting often find it easier to bring up what concerns them. They may begin to see the teacher as an 'ordinary' person who also talks about things other than school. A child, in the context of the family, sometimes shows another side which teachers have not seen before. Talking over a cup of tea or plate of food in someone's home can be much more relaxed than in the classroom or headteacher's room and allow discussions to be more intimate.

Home visits can, on the other hand, cause confusion when not properly thought out or when teachers are going in without genuine support from other members of staff. Tizard *et al.* (1981) found that home visiting is unpopular when 'the purpose of the visit is to complain about a child or to investigate family problems'. Tomlinson (1984), too, stresses the need to avoid the 'problem oriented approach'. Home–school liaison teachers who visit families occasionally can be caught in a difficult situation when they become the troubleshooters. Some have a particular brief to work with minority groups so that they can explain the work of the school and talk with parents about their concerns. They can find themselves marginalized, cast as the only one who is 'qualified' to work with these parents. Those who have a more general role but are sent out to visit families where there is a 'problem' can find themselves acting as a buffer where, in fact, individual teachers need to be involved in understanding the family circumstances. Visitors may also find themselves the go-between with other agencies. The more experienced will build up a network of available services and so may offer to make contacts for parents or even act as advocate in some situations. Such offers are extending the role of the teacher and they, as well as parents, need to be clear about where this begins and ends.

Many argue that it takes special skills to work with parents and that only a few should be allowed to go into homes. Certainly there are those who have a special ability or who are particularly interested in being involved with the adults as well as the children. But if certain teachers are designated as the ones who do all the work with adults then they can become isolated and frustrated. When other teachers appreciate the reasons for home visiting then it ceases to be a special 'scheme' and becomes an integral part of extending and improving home–school relations.

How information from the home is used is also crucial. Teachers may feel that they understand a family better once they have seen the cramped conditions children are living in or the house-proud parent or the books in the living room. But the danger of using this kind of 'evidence' to make judgements cannot be overemphasized. Much more important is the dialogue between parents and teachers. Home visiting is sometimes the start of a relationship which develops as teacher and parent get to know and understand each other better. Teachers can sometimes feel uneasy about things that they have been told in the privacy of the home and confidentiality can become an issue. They need to be very honest with parents so that they know, if information does go back to school, to whom it will go and how it will be used. It is vital, therefore, that teachers who do go in to homes have had a chance to look at their own values and prejudices so that they understand how these can affect the way that they relate to parents.

Preparing to visit

Why have you decided to visit?

Why will a meeting at someone's home be more advantageous than one in school? Is it because the parent is unlikely to be able to come to the school or because you can discuss things more easily there?

What is the underlying reason for the visit?

Is it to make acquaintance with the parents and child, to give or ask for information? There can easily be a hidden agenda when parents and teachers are not clear about the purpose. It is important to say if one has come on behalf of someone else like the classteacher. One should also give reasons if one is wanting specific information. Parents can feel extremely ill at ease when they find themselves giving answers to questions as if to a market researcher.

What sort of information are you wanting to give?

It could be about a special activity, school organization or something only relevant to this family. Whatever it is, one needs to be clear why it is better to talk about this in someone's home. One also needs to have thought carefully about how one will give parents the opportunity to ask for the information *they* consider important.

Are you there to get information from parents?

How do you think the parent will respond to this? What would you expect them to want to disclose to you? It is useful to think about how you would feel about giving information. Some parents will have had other 'visitors' such as the health visitor, social worker, or even the police. They may well wonder why you want to come as well. They may need assurance about how any information will be used and to whom it will go.

Will they want a visit from you?

Imagine that you are a parent. Think of some of the reasons why you may not want teachers to come to your home. If you are discussing this in a group speak in the first person. Here are a few examples:

> I don't want someone snooping around my house.
> Why the teacher? We've had enough people here what with the health visitor, the social worker and the insurance man.
> They should be at school teaching.
> They'll want to know if I've got any problems.
> They only come and find us when there's trouble.
> It's patronizing.
> They don't know what to talk about when they get here.

They come here with their lists to check up.
I feel embarrassed because I don't speak English.
They don't understand how we live.
School's the place you talk to teachers.

What do you see as being difficult for the teacher?

Some teachers feel shy, worry about whether to accept cups of tea, find it difficult talking with the television on or in front of other members of the family. These may seem minor things but are important to consider beforehand. Some teachers have come back surprised that everything has not stopped for them especially when they have made an appointment.

What will be the main advantage of this visit?

Look at it from the point of view of (a) the teacher, (b) the parent, (c) the child.

Organizing the visit

Who is the best person to visit?

There may be occasions when it is better for the classteacher to go rather than the home–school liaison teacher. If a parent speaks a little or no English, is it a good idea to take an interpreter? When there is specific information to pass on then this is obviously important but there are occasions when making acquaintance with a parent is disrupted by having a third party. Older children or other members of the family are often pleased to help out.

How will you let parents know that you are coming?

There are some advantages in just popping in to see families especially for full-time visitors or home–school liaison teachers who are known within the neighbourhood or have been several times. It makes the occasion informal, and 'neighbourly'. If one is carrying 'bad' news it may also be less threatening. But most teachers have limited time and a phone call or note beforehand explaining the reason for the visit is helpful. Some teachers get extremely annoyed when parents are not in even after this but it is important to bear in mind that not everyone's life is timetabled and a visit by the teacher may not be a priority!

How much time have you allowed for the visit?

Getting to know someone or sorting out children's problems takes time. One of the complaints parents have when they see teachers in school is that they do not get enough. Anyone visiting needs flexibility so that a discussion is not rushed. If one only has ten minutes to tell a parent about the school then this might be better done over the phone or by letter. The most important part of a home visit is giving parents time to ask questions and give their opinions.

What will you do when you get there?

Although one does not want to prescribe what is going to happen, it is surprising how vague some teachers are about why they are visiting. There is then general embarrassment and unease. If one knows there are young children then it may be helpful to take toys in for them. Certainly for preschool children, time spent with them is much appreciated by parents and children alike. Going in about a reading scheme gives a focus to the visit but it may also give rise to discussions about other things. There can be no vague notions about more 'friendly' relations or closer home–school links. Stepping out of school means leaving that organization behind and beginning to learn what is happening outside.

After the visit

How does the home visit help the teacher? This question is probably the hardest one of all but the most crucial one to ask. Many teachers will describe how privileged they feel to be welcomed into homes. On a general level, it gives them a chance to learn about different cultures and ways of bringing up children. Bringing information back to school helps get rid of stereotypes and preconceived ideas as teachers see for themselves the enormous variety of families.

But much more important, teachers will have to admit that they have needs, too. They are not there just to offer 'help'. Deciding to go to children's homes is asking to see or hear about them in their own personal sanctuaries and so gain information which one would not normally have access to. Going in to discuss a child who is not doing well at school involves looking at what the school, as well as the parent, is offering. Subconsciously or not, teachers may be wanting to know how to manage the child better. What they can find is that the parent is succeeding where they are failing – or vice versa. In any event, it has to be a sharing of information. A home visit helps with the unknowns and unresolved problems of teachers. As you begin to understand these better through listening and exchanging ideas, you are led not to ask how you can 'help', but rather how the parent can help you.

CHAPTER 11

Adult groups in school

This chapter concentrates on the kinds of group that run alongside the main school activities. They are notoriously difficult because there are often tensions between their underlying purpose and what actually happens. The enthusiastic head, opening the school up to the community with the offer of drop-in facilities or parent and toddler groups, can find the reality very different from the original vision. There is frequently disappointment when groups dwindle to a few regulars or when a parents' room is carefully prepared and no one seems to want to use it. Having groups in the classroom, such as coffee mornings for new entrants, can disrupt the normally calm atmosphere and put people off trying again. Yet they are an important resource when, in the words of one headteacher, they 'make the school open and welcome when otherwise there seems no reason for parents to come'.

There is much useful literature on group dynamics and group-work. But the very nature of these groups is that they are not formalized and people come and go. This is particularly difficult when teachers have imagined them as having some structure and educational input and envisage groups of parents running them themselves. Certainly we set out with this idea when opening up the South Harringay Preschool Centre. But what one finds is that before this can start happening, many parents want to relax, chat to each other and share individual concerns about bringing up their children. Understanding the importance of this opportunity for parents helps lessen the feeling of inadequacy when a group does not seem to be moving on as one would wish. Grant (1989) emphasizes the importance of teachers learning through experience, for, as she points out, people 'do not sit quietly, like the theorists' words, waiting for neat conclusions.' 'Life is not like school.'

There are teachers who enjoy being involved with adult groups but there will be others who have to be convinced of their benefits: some may never be. And if staff resent having adults in school then this can seriously undermine the group. Just as invitations to help in the classroom need to be part of school policy, so parent groups should also be regarded as one more facet of parental or community involvement. Teachers facilitating the groups often find themselves in a defensive position especially where there has either not been prior consultation or there is no opportunity for ongoing discussions with staff about what the group is achieving. It may be necessary to review its purpose regularly when it seems to disrupt routine or take valuable time away from teaching.

Douglas (1976) points out how 'people frequently join groups to achieve purposes other than those which are officially recognised'. This is not easy for teachers trained to plan in minute detail for children and looking for fairly immediate results. Watching a sewing group turn into a 'gossip shop' where people scream with laughter and never finish all that needs to be done can be extremely irritating. It can be worrying when cliques form or the group is apparently aimless. Making the decision either to intervene or to close a group is sometimes hard when people have begun to get to know each other. And changing the structure because it is not developing as one expects means that one can sometimes fall into the trap of driving people away because there are too many strictures. Heads find it hard when the response to invited speakers is poor and feel uncomfortable when asked for such events as tupperware parties. Requests for make-up sessions can be disillusioning if one is wanting to introduce the idea of women's rights. A community teacher spoke of her concern when bingo sessions were much greater crowd-pullers than meetings with an educational bias. She spoke of the tension between what parents might ask for and her professional judgement about what she should be providing.

These loose types of group for adults have the least connection with education in the formal sense yet may well be enabling adults to learn from each other, or indeed just relax. Thus the professional role of the teacher is stretched to the point of altruism. Giving groups space may mean that little ostensibly comes back into the school. It is like giving a gift, and some heads confess that allowing them to take place on the premises without being in direct control is difficult. Understanding what people are getting from a group is sometimes extremely hard. The consequences of adult interaction are not always as visible as that of children. Yet individuals may, and frequently are, getting valuable support from each other so it is important to check with them.

Parents' expectations of groups are often based on past experiences in school. They may well believe, like some teachers, that 'experts' should come in; thus, subconsciously, they may feel that they are expected to behave as they used to in the classroom, either giving their opinion when asked or to each other when the teacher is out of earshot. This may go some way to explaining why developing groups do sometimes go through stages of uncertainty or even disruptiveness. Working as social workers with groups of mothers in a school, Brown and Smith (1972) found, when they asked them about the usefulness of the group, that they were relieved at the informality and:

> frequently mentioned how refreshing it was to have their own discussion. In spite of our initial explanation about the structure of the group and its open ended content, the mothers came expecting a structured programme with speakers. Expectations were based on past experiences of more formal meetings . . .

Group dynamics

As teachers know from working with children, groups function differently depending on who is in them. Facilitating groups calls for a commitment to follow them through as they move on and change. People sometimes seem to believe that if parents are given a room, some chairs and a few toys all will go well. Yet having children may be the only thing they have in common and being part of a group can be difficult. I remember an apparently confident parent who, after having come regularly to the centre for about a year, remarked how she now felt able to say hello to newcomers and not worry about what to say after that. What many of the users appreciated most was that the workers, whatever they were doing, always looked up to greet them when they came in – a very small thing, but extremely important.

When a group is first starting there is the dilemma of wanting to make it very welcoming to everyone and also worrying about preferred ways of behaviour. Should one, for instance, exclude people, who may well be wanting to meet others, because they are chain smokers? This is an issue about which both parents and teachers have strong opinions and can never be ignored. What do you do about the small children who rush across the hall during PE? Or the children who cry when they see their mothers? It is the small practical difficulties which are usually the main cause for complaint, some of which need not arise if they have been thought out from the beginning.

Many parents using groups have small children. Classes in English as a second language for instance need good crèche facilities if the students are really going to be able to concentrate. Parents invited in to help, make books or get things ready for school events are frustrated when their children constantly want their attention. Yet the reality is that small children do not generally conform; they need supervision. It is not fair to complain because they run across the hall or cry loudly; it is better to be prepared!

Who takes responsibility and who organizes is another issue. Parents running groups voluntarily can easily find it becoming a burden if they feel staff are not interested. Other agencies such as social services, or adult education workers can be a source of annoyance to staff if they cannot see the benefits for themselves or the children.

Groups can sometimes get reputations, which are not deserved, for being for the 'needy' or, conversely, for a selected few who have certain skills such as sewing, or fund-raising ideas. This puts off other people from coming and it takes careful facilitating to open them up so that everyone feels welcome regardless of race or class or ability. Running closed groups is necessary sometimes where people have special concerns. Staff and other parents need to be clear why these have been set up so that they are seen as legitimate, not freakish or disruptive.

What is success?

Judging the success of groups may not be possible for some years. Sometimes people coming for support feel ambivalent about being part of a group; quite naturally, they do not want to feel that they are asking for help. Being with others may never appeal to some people but that is their choice, not necessarily the group's fault. Others seem to become too dependent or are only there to 'have a good moan'. They do not seem to appreciate this 'gift' from the school. Yet parents coming into the groups at the centre often only spoke about what they had gained from them afterwards.

People become more open as they get to know each other; this may lead to friendship and respect, but there is a possibility that it also brings conflict. Groups can break up, change or come to the end of their life cycle. The original purpose often changes when a group has been running for some time. For instance, a group which originally met to get to know each other may want to go on to do things for the school or have opportunities for their own self-development. This could mean excluding some people who do not want this or providing several groups. There can be times when the disadvantages seem to outweigh the advantages but those who are committed to them will work through these.

These groups are very different in nature from more organized activities such as parents' meetings and helping in class, and teachers who facilitate them can feel isolated – particularly when it seems as if neither parents nor teachers appreciate them. They sometimes wonder how they can justify their contribution but, as they frequently discover, it is important to have faith in 'being' rather than always 'doing'. Freire's (1972) idea of getting away from the 'banking' concept of education when the teacher deposits knowledge is relevant here, too. 'The efforts of a humanist, revolutionary educator' must, he writes, 'be imbued with a profound trust in men and their creative power'. Allowing groups of adults to use the school as they want, is in the first place, 'revolutionary'. Trusting them and then recognizing the 'creative power' that may come out of them is what makes them worthwhile.

Below are some of the negative and positive things that people have found who have run groups in school. They can be used as a starting point for discussion. Talking to others who are involved in this kind of work is particularly helpful so that one can share the experience and learn new skills.

Some difficulties

Numbers attending

People frequently do not turn up when they say they will. There are all sorts of reasons for this, not least that people sometimes feel that they have to say yes in the first place and then decide they really do not want to be involved. Numbers also fluctuate because of weather, family commitments, work, and other interests. Thus judging 'success' on numbers is spurious. It is what happens for people that is important.

Group behaviour

Smoking brings complaints either because there is too much or it is not possible. Schools have very different ways of dealing with this –

some banning it completely or having a smoking area away from the children. What facilitators find most successful is when a group itself is involved in the decision.

Clearing up is another bone of contention. Rooms left in a mess bring complaints from staff and parents. Rotas work in some schools but for some it is an ongoing problem which just has to be accepted and discussed regularly with the group. Making judgements about who are the main offenders only brings resentment.

Children's behaviour can be a source of tension and difficult for the parent whose child is not 'conforming'. Parents can feel extremely vulnerable when this happens and get angry or upset. Facilitators are often asked to come in as the 'authority' figure and this can create a dilemma when they seem to 'allow' behaviour that others would not. Some people believe that rules and regulations take away conflict and groups first forming may want to introduce many of these. People have strong views on 'discipline' and there need to be opportunities to talk about differences. Those who are finding their children 'difficult' will want support to work through situations rather than the kind of direct advice which is freely given and starts 'You should . . .'.

Exclusiveness not only happens because groups do not encourage others to come. It can also take place when loud conversations about people or sensitive issues dominate. 'Atmospheres' are created when people are expected to fit in with certain 'norms'. People who have become dependent on the group may resent newcomers.

Positive results

Children

Children get an opportunity to meet other adults and children and experience some of the activities which they will meet in school. Nursery and reception teachers often notice their confidence when they start school. People get to know others' children and see their own within a group setting and this furthers understanding of child development. Children in school begin to see it in broader educational terms, as a place for adults as well as themselves.

Adult participants

Many parents with young children feel isolated and it gives them opportunities to meet others and share experiences. An example of this was two mothers who had been living opposite each other for five years and did not know of each other's existence; their meeting developed into an important friendship. People begin to know who is in the neighbourhood and a network develops. These networks are important to the school, which can call on them for help and information.

Exchanging ideas and information and getting encouragement from others leads people both to further knowledge about bringing up their children and to self-knowledge. People also hear about courses and jobs. People have gone on to work in the community or in the school or have decided to take further training as a result of coming to these kinds of group.

Mixing with others whom they might not have met outside the school has given people a much greater understanding and has broken down prejudices and stereotypes. If children are being shown positive images in school but nothing changes at home then much of this work is invalidated. As adults meeting together have talked about, understood and valued the differences then equal opportunity policies – the words on paper – begin to take on more meaning.

People who have always found themselves on the receiving end of 'help and advice', have the chance to become active participants and to value their own wisdom. Davis (1985) stresses the importance of people being able to make contributions; 'the feeling of being able to help is vital since it is easier to receive help when you are giving'. And many of those facilitating and participating in the groups remark on how often people's self-esteem is raised.

The school

Having these groups can be uncomfortable and disrupting, particularly when parents, who have previously seemed quiet and compliant, become articulate and demanding. And it may seem easier to run the kind of group which fits into the more conventional idea of adult education. But education is about allowing people to find the relevant answers for themselves, to experience rather than be told, and, as those involved find, these groups can be of great significance, even a turning point for individuals. Perhaps Bruner's (1974) words sum up best: 'The courtesy of conversation', he writes 'may be the major ingredient in the courtesy of teaching.'

CHAPTER 12

Adults together

This book has focused on relationships between parents and teachers, but these do not take place in isolation. There are other adults with whom teachers need to work and communicate. There will be colleagues and governors as well as personnel from voluntary and statutory organizations. The quality of these relationships is often indicative of those that parents and teachers have with each other. Understanding the roles and responsibilities of each other is important if the gap between the 'caring' and 'educational' agencies is to be lessened. Getting away from the notion that the school – 'my school', as it is sometimes proprietorially known – is the centre of the universe can both take much of the stress away from teachers and introduce other valid views on the nature of education. The principles that apply in establishing good working relations with parents are the same: recognizing and valuing differences, breaking down preconceptions, and giving support to each other so that ultimately one can help the child.

It may seem hard to put further demands on teachers when it is difficult, or even impossible, for some to come out of the classroom and meet others. But it is important to know about the other activities which are happening in the neighbourhood if one is to be a source of information for parents and understand the context in which one is working. The idea of partnership is not exclusive to education. The Court Report (DHSS *et al*. 1976) urged professionals in health to 'see themselves as partners with parents'. Seebohm (1968) and Barclay (1982) highlighted the need for a community approach to social work so that families were regarded not just as recipients but also as having potential to change their own lives. The

Children Act 1989 calls for a greater partnership between parents and local authorities. Although the Act mainly affects social services and the courts, it calls for much greater liaison between services to provide for and protect children in need.

A multidisciplinary approach

Despite this common movement to work more closely with parents for the sake of children, most local services do not find themselves naturally working together. There have been some initiatives towards a multidisciplinary approach, particularly when working with under-fives, but these are not widespread. It is usually left to interested individual workers to make the contacts. And they find themselves coming up against the constraints of structures, funding and very different styles of management at both local and ministerial level.

Voluntary organizations sometimes hang on by the skin of their teeth; health visitors and social workers, like teachers, can be finding reorganization and new initiatives stressful when they are not involved in the initial planning. Services working at full stretch actually need to call upon each other. Yet the irony is, as Challis *et al.* (1988) point out, that 'when you need coordination most is when it is most difficult'. Initially, it is not only time-consuming but it also takes people away from other tasks.

Those who begin to work more closely with others become aware of common concerns. At an interdisciplinary course, where people began to learn about others' roles, there was a shock of recognition when a social worker described graphically the feelings she experienced and the pressures she was under. This was not done to gain sympathy or to make excuses. The teachers and health visitors were amazed at the similarities in their jobs where there were staff shortages and a lack of resources.

Few students get the opportunity for interdisciplinary discussions in their training or, indeed, ever meet anyone from other agencies, but it is here that a broader understanding could begin. Fletcher (1987) suggests that 'working with organized local people reveals a seething lava beneath the layers. The method of understanding is more difficult too. There are confusions and unanticipated consequences of action.' This can be off-putting for teachers who want to get on with the immediate task in the school, but to close one's self off from what is happening outside is to deny any possibility for change or additional support for parents, children or themselves.

Coming into school with a clearer view of its place amongst other organizations could go some way in removing some of the fear of getting involved in 'confusions and unanticipated consequences'.

Teachers cannot possibly be expected to provide everything. The demands for more day care for under-fives, out-of-school provision, and education for the elderly are increasing. The calls for community schools to provide opportunities 'from the cradle to the grave' can be overwhelming for even the most dedicated. Because 'education' is an all-embracing yet at the same time illusive word, schools can end up appearing to be the main providers. Teachers then complain because they believe that their role is being undermined and that schools just 'become an arm of the welfare state, taking the place, by order of the Government, of inadequate parents' (Sanders 1990). But where schools give up sole ownership of education, they move into a larger network outside the school, a network which offers new possibilities. Yet to find these possibilities there needs first to be a genuine recognition of others' contributions whether as childminders, playleaders, adult educators, supplementary schoolteachers or social workers. It may not mean meeting them regularly – although this will break down some of the misconceptions – but it does mean starting to provide a more co-ordinated, integral approach which takes account of what 'pupils', 'clients', and 'users' are asking.

How others see us

Stereotyping about other workers can be broken down. Teachers and social workers, for instance, commonly complain about each other. Teachers believe that social workers concentrate too much on the general workings of the family; social workers then say that teachers are too child-centred. Since they have little opportunity to meet, when they do it tends only to be at times of 'crisis' and therefore discussions between them are usually problem-orientated. Particularly when they are meeting about a child who is in trouble or has been abused, there are natural feelings of distress and possible inadequacy. Thus it is easy to want to blame or throw the responsibility on to others. Social workers often find themselves pushed into the role of 'dustbin', expected to find the final solution.

A problem-oriented approach affects parent–professional relationships. The case conference can be intimidating enough for workers if they do not know or trust each other; parents, increasingly invited to be 'part of the decision-making process', can find themselves isolated or put down. A parent introduced as 'mum' when everyone else was given a first name felt completely excluded from that moment on although 'they tried to be understanding'. Individual workers can find themselves forced into the position of the parents' advocate, defending them against the rest.

Workers in community groups feel put down by teachers sometimes. Schools are not always aware of their reputation of 'rich relation' who distributes largess when it is convenient. Many working without 'proper' qualifications in playgroups, out-of-school clubs or community projects speak of the inferior position in which they sometimes feel themselves and their resentment when they are regarded as a peripheral service. This attitude is not always the school's intention. One teacher was shocked when a colleague in a community group with whom she had developed a close working relationship over many years said that she still felt her opinion was not as valid as hers because she did not have a teacher's qualification. This was not because the teacher had put herself in this superior position. But it highlights the great divide between schools and outsiders which has to be overcome. Like parents, workers also have had their own personal experiences of school as children; these can often be hard to forget.

Even those working within the education service itself but outside the school can find themselves out on a limb. Jones (1986) stresses the need for support and contact for community teachers who can otherwise feel like 'introspective missionaries'. The Thomas Report (ILEA 1985) on primary schools suggested that adult education could have a role in helping 'parents to understand better what schools are doing'. An adult educator expressed the view that since much of the emphasis for involving parents in school was now on tackling underachievement, a large part of parent education was being ignored. Adult education could help parents 'examine attitudes and potential for change'. Without close co-operation with the schools, this change, as she realized, could easily lead them into conflict. Those working in parent groups outside school find themselves in this position and it needs much trust between them and teachers if they are not to remain merely an isolated place for parents to express their views.

Davie (1977) highlights the divisions between agencies because of language. 'They learn their own specialised vocabularies and their own restricted codes', he writes. 'More importantly their framework of professional concepts will differ quite markedly, so that sometimes even the same words can have different meanings or connotations.' Having worked in both education and social services departments, I know how easy it is to feel excluded when one does not speak the same language. Asking can bring looks of astonishment when it is taken for granted that you understand the management structure or the latest initials for a new innovation. It takes considerable courage at any meeting, let alone inter-agency ones, to ask what someone is talking about, but phrases such as 'INSET', 'integrated day', 'key stages', all so much a part of teachers' vocabulary, mean nothing to the uninitiated. Jones *et al.* (1983) draw attention to social workers' use of such phrases as 'presenting problems' and 'client self-determination' which mean a great deal to them but which are packed with implications which others may not understand. Being with medical personnel brings another whole host of words. Sometimes the different use of language may highlight the different way of looking at things; this can be illuminating and educative. But it is important to consider how parents can receive a coherent and helpful message if the 'professionals' themselves do not understand each other!

So why get together?

Many feeling hard pressed with all there is to do at school, still have to be convinced that working in an interdisciplinary way is worthwhile. Yet if they work with parents in a more equal and open way, this will mean barriers breaking and old ways changing. Below I list in general terms some of the benefits that I see in working together. In practice, you are likely to find others.

- Different viewpoints bring new meanings and new possibilities.
- Children will be influenced by many different adults. If the school's views are very different from the ones they meet outside they will cease to have relevance.
- Joint action on common problems has much greater possibility of success than unco-ordinated action.
- Duplicating effort and resources is a waste of everybody's time and energy.
- Barriers between departments and services exist at the upper levels of administration. Workers and parents together have a stronger voice and message.
- Services and agencies become more open and accessible to those that need them. They get rid of 'problem' or 'them and us' cultures.

- Changing old patterns can mean taking a risk. Involving other adults in the planning and decisions is much more likely to bring success.
- Getting rid of rituals and stereotypes is a move to a more equal and open partnership.
- Sharing resources, skills and knowledge gives children a broader view of education and the understanding that learning does not just take place at school.

As we become increasingly aware of the close relationship between our planet and ourselves and the way we have caused so much destruction and fragmentation, then it must be important to give our children a more holistic approach to education. We can begin doing this in a very small way, as we collaborate more closely, develop joint enterprises and share different viewpoints. There will be times when we are frustrated, angry and downcast as we come across barriers or cope with change. But if the main reason for getting together, as parents and teachers or as working colleagues, is to benefit the child, then in the words of the I Ching:

The movement is natural, arising spontaneously. For this reason the transformation of the old becomes easy. The old is discarded and the new is introduced. Both measures accord with time; therefore no harm results.

Bibliography

Aldrich, R. and Leighton, P. (1985) *Education: Time for a New Act*, Bedford Way Papers 23, University of London Institute of Education.

Atkin, J. and Bastiani, J. (1985) *Preparing Teachers to Work with Parents – A Survey of Initial Training*, University of Nottingham School of Education.

Bacon, W. (1978) *Public Accountability and the Schooling System*, Harper & Row.

Back, K. and Back, K. (1982) *Assertiveness at Work*, McGraw-Hill.

Barclay, P. (1982) *Social Workers: Their Roles and Tasks*, National Institute of Social Work/Bedford Square Press.

Bastiani, J. (1989) *Working with Parents. A Whole School Approach*, NFER-Nelson.

Becher, T., Eraut, M. and Knight, J. (1981) *Policies for Educational Accountability*, Heinemann.

Bernstein, B. (1970) 'Education cannot compensate for society', *New Society*, 26 February.

Bernstein, B. (1971) *Class Codes and Control*, vol. 1, Routledge & Kegan Paul.

Bowlby, J. (1953) *Child Care and the Growth of Love*, Penguin.

Bronfenbrenner, U. (1974) *Is Early Intervention Effective? A Report on Longitudinal Evaluations of Pre-school Programs*, vol. 2, Department of Health Education and Welfare, Office of Child Development, Washington, DC.

Brown, L. and Smith, J. (1972) 'Groups for mothers', *Social Work Today*, vol. 3, no. 10, quoted in Douglas (1976).

Bruner, J. (1974) *The Relevance of Education*, Penguin.

Challis, L., Fuller, S., Henwood, M., Klein, R., Plowden, W., Webb, A., Whittingham, P. and Wistow, G. (1988) *Joint Approaches to Social Policy. Rationality and Practice*, Cambridge University Press.

Children's Committee (1980) *The Needs of Under Fives in the Family*, The Children's Committee, Mary Ward House, 5–7 Tavistock Place, London WC1 9SS.

Council of Local Education Authorities (1978) *Conditions of Service for Schoolteachers in England & Wales* (Burgundy Book), CLEA/ST.

Cyster, R., Clift, P. S. and Battle, S. (1979) *Parental Involvement in Primary Schools*, NFER Publishing Co.

Davie, R. (1977) 'The interface between education and social services' quoted in Davie (1985) 'Equalities and inequalities in working together for children' in E. De'Ath and G. Pugh (eds), *Partnership Papers 6*, National Children's Bureau.

Davis, H. (1985) 'Developing the role of parent adviser in the child health service' in E. De'Ath and G. Pugh, (eds) *Partnership Papers 3*, National Children's Bureau.

Davis, W. (1989) 'Plea of a potential ally' *Times Educational Supplement*, 8 December, p. 20.

Department of Education and Science (1967) *Children and their Primary Schools* (Plowden Report), HMSO.

Department of Education and Science (1972) *Education: a Framework for Expansion*, Cmnd 5174, HMSO.

Department of Education and Science (1975) *A Language for Life* (Bullock Report), HMSO.

Department of Education and Science (1981) *West Indian Children in Our Schools: Interim Report of the Committee of Inquiry into the Education of Children from Ethnic Minority Groups* (Rampton Report), HMSO.

Department of Education and Science (1984) *Parental Influence at School*, Cmnd 9242, HMSO.

Department of Education and Science (1985a) *Education for All* (Swann Report), Cmnd 9453, HMSO.

Department of Education and Science (1985b) *Better Schools*, Cmnd 9469, HMSO.

Department of Education and Science (1989a) *Our Changing Schools*: A Handbook for Parents, HMSO.

Department of Education and Science (1989b) Circular 17/89, The Education (School Records) Regulation 1989, HMSO.

Department of Health and Social Security, Department of Education and Science, and Welsh Office (1976) *Fit for the Future* (Court Report), Cmnd 6684, HMSO.

Dickson, A. (1982) *A Woman in Your Own Right*, Quartet.

Douglas, J. (1964) *The Home and the School*, MacGibbon & Kee.

Douglas, T. (1976) *Groupwork Practice*, Tavistock.

Edwards, V. and Redfern, A. (1988) *At Home in School*, Routledge.

Egan, G. (1986) *The Skilled Helper*, Brooks/Cole.

Elliott, J., Bridges, D., Ebutt, D., Gibson, R. and Nias, J. (1981) *School Accountability*, Grant McIntyre.

Farquhar, C., Blatchford, P., Burke, J., Plewis, I. and Tizard, B. (1985) 'A comparison of the views of parents and reception teachers', *Education 3–13*, vol. 13, no. 2, pp. 17–22.

Finch, J. (1983) 'Can skills be shared? Preschool playgroups in disadvantaged areas', *Community Development Journal*, vol. 18, no. 3, pp. 251–6.

Fletcher, C. (1987) 'The meanings of community in community education' in G. Allen, J. Bastiani, I. Martin and K. Richards (eds), *Community Education. An Agenda for Educational Reform*, Open University Press.

Fletcher, C. (1989) 'Towards empowerment in community education' in C. Harber and R. Meighan (eds), *The Democratic School: Educational Management and the Practice of Democracy*, Education Now Publishing Cooperative.

Freire, P. (1972) *Pedagogy of the Oppressed*, Pelican.

Froebel, F. (1887) *The Education of Man*, Sidney Appleton.

Gibbons, C. (1987) 'A distinct disadvantage', *Times Educational Supplement*, 13 November.

Golby, M. (1989) 'Parent governorship in the new order' in F. Macleod (ed) *Parents and Schools: the Contemporary Challenge*, Falmer.

Grant, D. (1989) *Learning Relations*, Routledge.

Griffith, A. and Hamilton, D. (1984) *Parent, Child, Teacher. Working together in Children's Learning*, Methuen.

Halsey, A. (1972) *Educational Priority. EPA Problems and Policies*, vol. 1, HMSO.

Handy, C. and Aitken, R. (1986) *Understanding Schools as Organizations*, Penguin.

Hewison, J. (1981) 'Home is where the help is', *Times Educational Supplement*, 16 January.

Hughes, M., Wikeley, F. and Nash, T. (1990) 'Business partners', *Times Educational Supplement* , 5 January, pp. 20–1.

Inner London Education Authority (1984) *Improving Secondary Schools: Report of the Committee on the Curriculum and Organisation of Secondary Schools* (Hargreaves Report), ILEA.

Inner London Education Authority (1985) *Improving Primary Schools: Report of the Committee on Private Education* (Thomas Report), ILEA.

Jackson, A. and Hannon, P. (1981) *The Bellfield Reading Project*, Bellfield Community Council, Rochdale.

Jackson, B. and Marsden, D. (1962) *Education and the Working Class*, Routledge & Kegan Paul.

Jones, K., Brown, J. and Bradshaw, J. (1983) *Issues in Social Policy*, rev. edn, Routledge & Kegan Paul.

Jones, S. (1986) 'The community teacher: learning the role from initiatives', *Journal of Community Education*, vol. 5, no. 1, pp. 23–6.

Kelly, G. (1955) *The Psychology of Personal Constructs*, Norton, New York.

Lodge, B. (1989a) 'Shower of gifts entices parents', *Times Educational Supplement*, 3 November, p. 1.

Lodge, B. (1989b) 'Survey highlights parents' ignorance about reforms', *Times Educational Supplement*, 8 December.

Macbeth, A. (1984) *The Child Between – A Report on School–Family Relations in the Countries of the European Community*, Office for Official Publication of the European Communities, Luxembourg.

Macbeth, A. (1988) 'A minimum programme and signed understanding' in M. Woodhead and A. McGrath (eds), *Family, School and Society*, Hodder & Stoughton.

Macleod, F., (ed.) (1989) *Parents and Schools: the Contemporary Challenge*, Falmer.

Midwinter, E. (1972) *Priority Education*, Penguin.

Midwinter, E. (1977) *Education for Sale*, Penguin.

Milward, V. (1983) 'Romanticism and pessimism: community education and women', *School Organisation*, vol. 3, no. 4, pp. 403–10.

Moncur, A. (1985) 'Unpaid school helpers worry teachers', *The Guardian*, 10 January.

Morgan, D. (1981) 'Men, masculinity and the process of sociological enquiry' in H. Roberts (ed.) *Doing Feminist Research*, Routledge & Kegan Paul.

Mulvaney, M. (1984) 'The impact of an anti-racist policy in the school community' in M. Straker-Welds (ed.) *Education for a Multicultural Society*, Bell & Hyman.

Munn, P. (1988) 'Accountability and parent–teacher communication' in A. Cohen (ed.) *Early Education: The Parents' Role*, (1988) Paul Chapman.

Musgrove, F. and Taylor, P. (1969) *Society and the Teacher's Role*, Routledge & Kegan Paul.

National Union of Teachers (1987) *Pupils, Teachers and Parents*, NUT.

National Union of Teachers (1989) *Anti-racism in Education Guidelines*, NUT.

Newson, J. and Newson, E. (1976) *Seven Years Old in the Home Environment*, Allen & Unwin.

Newson, J. and Newson, E. *Perspectives on School at Seven Years Old*, Allen & Unwin.

O'Hagan, B. (1986) 'Heads versus tutors: a conflict of values', *Journal of Community Education*, vol. 5, no. 1, pp. 21–2.

Pendleton, D., Schofield, T., Tate, P. and Havelock, P. (1984) *The Consultation. An Approach to Learning and Teaching*, Oxford University Press.

Poulton, G. (1983) 'Origins and development of pre-school home visiting' in G. Aplin and G. Pugh (eds) *Perspectives on Pre-School Home Visiting*, National Children's Bureau and Community Education Development Centre.

Pugh, G., Aplin, G., De'Ath, E. and Moxon, M. (1987) *Partnership in Action*, vols 1 and 2, National Children's Bureau.

Pugh, G. and De'Ath, E. (1984) *The Needs of Parents*, National Children's Bureau.

Roberts, K. (1980) 'Schools, parents and social class' in M. Craft, J. Raynor, and H. Cohen, (eds), *Linking Home and School*, 3rd edn, Harper & Row.

Sallis, J. (1986) 'The listening school: parents and the public' in M. Wood-head, and A. McGrath (1988) (eds), *Family, School and Society*, Hodder and Stoughton.

Sanders, J. (1990) 'Hard knocks on the road to discovery', *The Guardian*, 20 February.

Seebohm, F. (1968), *Report of the Committee on Local Authority and Allied Personal Social Services*, Cmnd 3703, HMSO.

Silverman, D. and Stacey, M. (1989) 'Listen to the parents', *Special Children*, no. 27, pp. 18–19.

Smith, G. (ed.) (1975) *Educational Priority, – Vol. 4. EPA. The West Riding Project*, HMSO.

Smith, T., (1980) *Parents and Preschool*, Grant McIntyre.

Steedman, C. (1988) '"The mother made conscious": the historical development of a primary school pedagogy' in M. Woodhead, and A. McGrath (1988) (eds) *Family, School and Society*, Hodder and Stoughton.

Stone, M. (1981) *The Education of the Black Child in Britain*, Fontana.

Theodoulou, T. (1989) 'Does the father have a role in nursery centres?' unpublished major module for CSS course.

Tizard, B. and Hughes, M. (1984) *Young Children Learning – Talking and Thinking at Home and School*, Fontana.

Tizard, B., Mortimore, J. and Burchell, B. (1981) *Involving Parents in Nursery and Infant Schools*, Grant McIntyre.

Tomlinson, S. (1984) *Home and School in Multicultural Britain*, Batsford.

Tough, J. (1973) *Focus on Meaning*, Allen & Unwin.

Tough, J. (1979) *Talk for Teaching and Learning*, Schools Council.

Watt, J. (1988) 'Early education and the community' in A. Cohen, (ed.) *Early Education: the Parents' Role*, Paul Chapman.

Weinberger, J., Jackson, A. and Hannon, P. (1986) 'Involving parents in the teaching of reading. Will they respond?', *Reading*, vol. 20, no. 3, November.

Wells, G. (1978) 'Talking with children: the complementary roles of parents and teachers', *English in Education*, vol. 12, no. 2, pp. 15–36.

Woodhead, M. and McGrath, A. (eds) (1988) *Family, School and Society*, Hodder and Stoughton.

Wragg, T. (1989) 'Parent power' in F. Macleod (ed.) *Parents and Schools: the Contemporary Challenge*, Falmer.

Young, M. and McGeeney, P. (1968) *Learning Begins at Home*, Routledge & Kegan Paul.

Index